COUNTRY LIVING

Cozy Knits for Cuddly Babies

COUNTRY LIVING

Cozy Knits for Cuddly Babies

ELANOR LYNN

HEARST BOOKS

A DIVISION OF STERLING PUBLISHING CO., INC.

NEW YORK

JACKET AND INTERIOR BOOK DESIGN BY DEBORAH KERNER, DANCING BEARS DESIGN
FRONT COVER PHOTOGRAPHY BY JACK DEUTSCH
BACK COVER PHOTOGRAPHY BY JACK DEUTSCH AND JOESEPH KUGIELSKY
ILLUSTRATIONS BY CAROL RUZICKA
TECHNICAL EDITING AND COPYEDITING BY ELLEN LIBERLES
EDITORIAL CONSULTING AND PHOTO STYLING BY CAROL SPIER

Library of Congress Cataloging-in-Publication Data
Lynn, Elanor.
Country living cozy knits for cuddly babies / Elanor Lynn.
p. cm.
Includes index.
ISBN 1-58816-435-7
1. Knitting—Patterns. 2. Infants' clothing. I. Title: Cozy knits for cuddly babies.
II. Country living (New York, N.Y.) III. Title.
TT825.L96 2005
746.43'20432--dc22
2005000829

10 9 8 7 6 5 4 3 2 1

Published by Hearst Books
A Division of Sterling Publishing Co., Inc.
387 Park Avenue South, New York, NY 10016

Country Living is a trademark of Hearst Communications, Inc.

www.countryliving.com

For information about custom editions, special sales, premium and corporate purchases,
please contact Sterling Special Sales Department at 800-805-5489 or specialsales@sterlingpub.com.

Distributed in Canada by Sterling Publishing
c/o Canadian Manda Group, 165 Dufferin Street
Toronto, Ontario, Canada M6K 3H6

Distributed in Australia by Capricorn Link (Australia) Pty. Ltd.
P.O. Box 704, Windsor, NSW 2756 Australia

Manufactured in China
ISBN 1-58816-435-7

For Sean

Acknowledgements

This book has been shaped by the influence of many gifted and generous people, especially my students. There are a few students I would like to thank in particular: Eiko Berkowitz, Jane Kornbluh, Riene Hewitt, Maggie Trakas, Natalie Reeves, Kevin Lai, Kelley Abate, and Loree Lash, among many others. Another student I would like to thank is Nancy Soriano, editor of *Country Living Magazine*; she is the reason this book exists. Her interest in my work led me to Jacqueline Deval at Hearst Books, to whom I owe much gratitude for inviting me to join the Sterling family and for her help in developing *Cozy Knits for Cuddly Babies*.

Maryanne Bannon is the editor of my dreams. Her insight, creativity, experience, gentle guidance, and patience have made every step an absolute pleasure. She also assembled an amazing group to transform the manuscript into a living, breathing book. They include art director Celia Fuller, designer Deborah Kerner, assistant designer Margaret Rubiano, copy editor Ellen Liberles, and assistant project editor Catharine Wells. Maryanne also brought in Carol Spier, former editor of *Threads* magazine, as consulting editor and photo stylist. She and Jack Deutsch and Joseph Kugielsky, our photographers, are responsible for making this book so beautiful. In addition to working closely with Carol Ruzicka, the talented illustrator, Carol brought to the book many excellent technical and artistic suggestions. I would especially like to thank the delightful models and their moms, dads, grandmas, and nannies who accompanied them to the photo shoot. Maryanne engaged Chris O'Shea, an expert "baby wrangler," whose dynamic method efficiently brought out the best in each child.

There are many other people I must thank for their encouragement and enthusiasm, starting with my teachers: Mrs. Geisler, Marjorie Janes, Danny Michaelson, Martha Wittman, Susan Sgorbati, Liz Dearing, Rhoda Carroll, Eddie Stern, and Sifu Joseph Demundo. I would also like to thank G. Roy Levin, Carolyn Shapiro, and Jessica Lutz of Vermont College's MFA in Visual Art program. I am very grateful to Jonathan Bee, who invited me to found Purls of Hope at Children's Hope Foundation. Rita Bobry of Downtown Yarns deserves my profound appreciation for creating a hothouse where I had the chance to meet and work with an eclectic array of knitters and crocheters. I offer a special thanks to Lela Nargi, for inviting me to contribute to *Living with Knitting* (2006, Voyager). Pam Chmiel at Klatch, Alison Ferst at Children's Hope Foundation, Stitches East, Gilda's Club, the Thompson Square Middle School and Charles R. Morris have all contributed to this book. Joan Sommerville, the "Yarn Goddesss" at Cascade Yarns amply deserves the title; she made the process of selecting and procuring the yarn for the projects effortless. I am very proud to endorse Cascade Yarns as an American manufacturer and distributor of fine yarns. Finally, my deepest thanks are to my Mom for teaching me how to knit and to my Dad for teaching me how to design and build things. "Measure twice, cut once."

Contents

Foreword

I had been thinking about learning to knit for several years before I actually got started. What appealed to me was its quiet process of being active. I've often thought of knitting as a type of creative meditation. The biggest challenge for me was just making the time to go to a yarn shop to get the materials and, most of all, to receive some guidance. Several editors at *Country Living* had recently started to knit and told me about a lovely shop in downtown Manhattan. I called the shop and inquired if anyone from the shop's staff would be open to coming to my office to give me a knitting class (I knew my schedule wouldn't permit me to get downtown). They said yes, there was someone, and she would give me a call. That person was Elanor Lynn. We spoke on the phone and met two weeks later at my office after the work day. When I met Elanor in person, she was sitting in the waiting area knitting and reading—simultaneously. A petite woman with blonde hair, glasses, and bright red lipstick, Elanor made knitting look so easy. And she continues to do that to this day. I was fortunate to have Elanor as my instructor. She is not only an artist whose medium is fiber—she's also a teacher at heart. Elanor is passionate about knitting and seeks to share that spirit and knowledge. She has the artistic and technical ability to combine wonderfully complex textures and colors in her knitting as well as to make the most simple of projects equally exciting and important. I'm delighted to bring you Elanor's first book, *Cozy Knits for Cuddly Babies*. In this book she'll take you through each project and pattern step by step in a way that will make knitting not only attainable but fun—as she did for me in my first lesson and thereafter.

Nancy Mernit Soriano

• • •

Editor in Chief, Country Living

Introduction

My Mom taught me to knit on my sixth birthday. She was good with her hands and always found time to make attractive garments for our family and accessories for our home. I loved watching her work—constructing practical and beautiful things through the arts of crochet, weaving, sewing, gardening, and cooking. As a curious five-year old I was fascinated most by knitting and I was desperate to learn. My Mom said I had to wait until I was six, so I watched her knit through the eternity of a Northeast winter until the last patches of snow melted in mid-May. Earlier that week we had made an expedition to town for big needles and thick yarn. Montpelier's lone ladies' wear shop on Main Street stocked a few basic yarns in a thrilling range of vibrant colors.

On the morning of my birthday I had to wait until after breakfast and the opening of presents before my lesson. Finally, we sat in a pool of sunlight on the Persian carpet in the living room of our cabin set deep in the woods of Vermont to begin my first lesson. First, we wound the skein of heavy yellow rug wool into a ball. Next, my Mom cast on 12 stitches and knit the first row for me. I watched her make the stitches and was transfixed by the moment when the new stitch on the right needle passed through the old stitch on the left needle. My turn. Nervous and excited, I held the needles and waited. Nothing happened. I was confused and frustrated because my hands did not instantly and automatically know what to do. My Mom patiently guided me, hand over hand, for the first few rows. Suddenly, it clicked. Knitting felt like flying.

When engaged in the act of making something, whether knitting or crocheting, chopping wood or vegetables, playing an instrument or a sport, many people report losing track of time and an increased sense of well-being. Someday, scientific research will prove that knitting and other fine-motor, hand-eye coordinated activities have profound and diverse benefits. For now, anecdotal evidence shows that needlework provides a much-needed, relaxing, and creative outlet. It is not an exaggeration to say that knitting has changed my life. I've seen it bring untold joy and satisfaction to countless knitters of all descriptions and backgrounds. What we share is a love of seeing raw materials transformed into useful and attractive items for those we love. The mystery of knitting is that by manipulating two pointy sticks you can turn string into nearly anything you can imagine.

My work used to be focused on making obsessively complex and precisely executed designs. In the last decade, I have developed a deep respect for what some call "mistakes"; I prefer to call these "design opportunities." These may include running out of yarn and completing a sweater with an unplanned color, knits or purls in unintended places, a cable twisted the "wrong" way or a lace pattern gone askew. As the author of your knitting, when these mistakes occur, you have the choice of either going back and fixing them or continuing on and leaving the "accident" in place. You may choose to leave in a thick slub of yarn as a reminder of the crisp autumn day you spent laughing and catching up with a dear friend at the park. In this way your knitting can function as a diary, a non-verbal narrative document of your life. "Mess-ups" present the possibility of creating something without exerting control over every aspect. A "perfect" flower or leaf is a charming stylization of nature. However, by varying your shaping and stitches you create an organic plant with a more life-like structure and appearance. My recent work includes randomly turned cables that mimic complex intertwined vines. The level of perfectionism you apply to your work is your decision. Many craft traditions honor the inclusion of at least one purposeful flaw in each article. The demands of everyday life are sufficiently taxing; your knitting should be a respite from, not the cause of stress.

More than thirty years after my first lesson, I now realize that my Dad, a master carpenter who specializes in eccentric buildings, has been as great an influence on my knitting as my Mom. From watching him practice his craft, I learned how to measure, design, draw and build both garments and sculptural objects. Now I live in Brooklyn, New York, and I do most of my gardening by knitting and crocheting natural forms such as flowers, trees, snakes, fish, water, rocks, artichokes, radishes, and onions as stuffed objects and tapestries. I also enjoy knitting sweaters, socks, hats, bags, and scarves. As a designer and teacher, my goal is to create patterns that offer the best results with the least effort while increasing your vocabulary of skills. I created each of the projects in this book with you in mind, with the hope that you will feel I am by your side, talking you through each step. These patterns are for you; they are not about what I can knit, they are about what you can knit.

Many of my students are motivated to learn to knit or re-learn the craft by the arrival of a new baby and what could be a better inspiration? The small scale of baby knits provides quick results for those on tight schedules. Look for tips on how several of the garments in this book can be adapted to adult sizes. You will find hats, booties, and blankets that will keep babies warm not just in body. With the time, energy, and love you invest, each project you make will be a treasured heirloom.

Keep knitting.

• • •

Elanor Lynn

How to Use This Book

Part One, The Course, will teach you (or review for you) the fundamentals of knitting: casting on and binding off, knitting and purling, increasing and decreasing, and avoiding common bungles.

The projects in Part Two are arranged in order of increasing complexity. The projects are designed to be flattering, easy to knit and finish, and to introduce you to the basics of knitting. As an added bonus, many of the patterns can be adapted to larger sizes with only slight adjustments. The first three projects are designed to give you a chance to practice basic knitting while making an afghan, a pair of ribbed knee pads, and a textured poncho. Among the other projects are hats knit in the round, a bunny bonnet and booties, knit-top sundresses with fabric skirts, a top-down striped pullover that you can lengthen with "rings" as the child grows, super-simple socks, and sweet blankets.

If you are a new knitter, practice knitting and purling, increasing and decreasing, and you will be ready to tackle any project in the book. Read carefully, with knitting in hand, and be patient with yourself. You can accomplish anything you wish including cables, color work, and expert finishing. Follow the patterns precisely and your projects will come out like those pictured. However, I hope you—whether novice or experienced—will consider the patterns as collaborative frameworks with which you can begin to create your own designs.

Together, the course and the projects will give new knitters the confidence to experiment with lots of different kinds of knitting. Consider the projects as learning tools to discover what kind of knitting you enjoy most. And of course, if knitting comes easily to you, just choose the project that appeals most to you, and enjoy.

Sizing

Most of the garments are given in three sizes: small for 3-6 months, medium for 6-12 months, and large for 12-18 months. Within the directions for a project, you will see numbers written in sets; for example, "cast on 63 (73, 75) sts." This means to work the first set of numbers for the smallest size and the subsequent sets in parentheses for the progressively larger sizes. Babies vary greatly in size and correct fit is fairly subjective, depending on whether the garment is desired to fit tightly or loosely. Be sure to knit to the gauge given, adjusting needle sizes if needed. If you want an oversized garment or if you tend to knit tightly you may wish to make the next larger size as the baby will grow into the garment. All garments are shown in the smallest size, unless indicated otherwise.

Gauge

Gauge is given over 4 inches on the main needle size in stockinette stitch unless otherwise indicated. See page 44 for a complete discussion of how to measure gauge accurately.

Yarn

When knitting for babies and children, consult with the parents regarding fiber choice. Some parents want only natural fibers on their baby's skin while others prefer the ease of super-wash wool and/or synthetic yarns. All the samples in the book are knit with Cascade Yarns, which are widely available in the U.S. and Canada (Appendix B, page 139). If you would like to substitute another yarn, select one of a similar weight and be sure to check yardage carefully; it's best not to be caught short.

Needles

All the projects in this book were knitted on circular or double-pointed needles. Unless circular needles are specified, you can work on short or long straight needles, if you prefer.

Following Instructions

Some knitters find it worth taking the time to translate the condensed information of patterns into their own words. Check through the pattern before you

photocopy of project instructions so you can make notes as you knit while keeping a clean original as a back-up copy. Like most knitters, you will likely give away much of your handwork as gifts for loved ones. Not only is it very satisfying to look back through your notes and recall the contented hours you spent planning and knitting your original creations, but you'll have a record of that baby sweater your best friend treasures, the gorgeous yarn you loved, the quandaries solved, and the techniques mastered to mix and match for new creations.

begin, looking up any abbreviations you don't understand in Appendix A (page 137) and marking any steps you aren't sure about. When you approach the steps in sequence, with knitting in hand, the instructions will most likely make sense in the context of what you are doing.

Keeping a Project Journal

Start a project binder and save yarn labels, a snip of the yarn, and notes on the projects that you complete (see the sample in Appendix C, page 140). Make a

Getting Started

While it is possible to knit on any kind of stick, even chopsticks and pencils, and use any kind of string, knitting tools and gadgets are irresistible implements. If your budget permits, invest in the best materials and tools you can find. However, the only necessities are yarn, needles, and a yarn needle (large-eyed sewing needle). Everything else can be improvised: safety pins and paper clips for stitch markers, pencil and paper for row counters, tapestry needle and yarn for stitch holders.

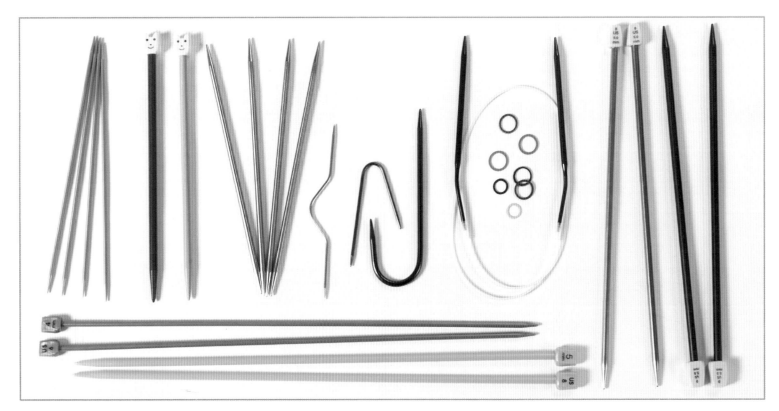

Novelty yarns have become phenomenally popular in the past few years and now take up considerable space in most yarn shops. These yarns include glitzy and flashy "eyelash," ribbon, and "slubbed" varieties. Beware, these yarns do produce beautiful results but also make for slower knitting. The good news for new knitters is that the fancy texture, while making it more difficult to see your stitches during knitting, has the advantage of camouflaging any irregularities in your work. Generally, novelty yarns are best suited for simple scarves and projects with little shaping.

Yarn

Yarn today comes in a wonderful array of colors and a variety of natural and synthetic fiber choices including wool, alpaca, cashmere, mohair, llama, angora, cotton, rayon, hemp, silk, nylon, acrylic, and other synthetics and blends. Always consider the intended wearer when selecting yarn; it is best to inquire about wool allergies before investing so much of your time in the knitting. Unless special effects or needs are in order, select a high quality wool or wool blend for most of your projects; wool is the easiest of all fibers to work in and worth any extra effort to care for. Wool has superior elasticity, durability, and the most charming smell when damp.

The other basic factor is weight. From finest to thickest, standard yarn weights are: laceweight, fingering or baby, sport, worsted, aran, bulky, and chunky. For practice purposes, new knitters should select a worsted or bulky weight yarn.

With worsted yarn, I recommend U.S. needle sizes 7 to 9 (4.5-5.5mm), and for bulky yarn, U.S. sizes 10 to 11 (6-8mm). Ideally, you should practice with both to find out which you prefer. The bulkier yarn and thicker needles yield bigger stitches so you can create your fabric faster. The thinner yarn and needles are easier to manipulate but require a bit more patience since it takes more stitches and rows to make the same amount of material.

Most yarn comes ready to knit in pull-skeins or balls. Remove the label and set aside for your project journal. Some yarns need to be wound into balls before you can start knitting. If you are not certain, ask when you purchase your yarn. Some shops will even wind it into a ball for you. If not, ask for instructions on winding the yarn yourself.

"Always buy an extra ball." This is your insurance policy, covering the possibility of running out of yarn, especially when making an adult sweater. Check with your yarn shop about their exchange policy before you buy. Most will be happy to give you store credit as long as the yarn is in resalable condition and in-season. Avoid running short unless you welcome unplanned design opportunities.

Yarn shops are great resources —and not just for yarn. Most yarn shops are glad to help their customers, whether to select yarns for a new project or give help for completing a project. Find one you like and develop a good rapport with the sales staff. Most shops offer lessons for beginners and a variety of project classes. As a customer or a student, you will find others who share a common love of fiber and color and the endless ways it can be interconnected. Group classes offer the opportunity to learn from an expert and from the students in your class. You can pick up tips and refine your style by watching others knit. Also look for unique handmade yarns at your local farmer's market.

Needles

There are many kinds of needles available and it doesn't matter what kind you choose because you can adapt your knitting to whatever you have available. If you are a new knitter, bamboo and plastic needles give you more control. They are also more likely to pass unpredictable airline security regulations (always bring a mailer with you, just in case). Metal needles tend to be slippery and therefore are usually favored by fast knitters. I knit almost exclusively on 16- and 24-inch long Addi Turbo circular needles, even for flat knitting. The circular needle also acts a holder when making top-down sweaters. While some people prefer long straight needles that can be tucked under the arms or otherwise supported, I prefer the narrower working profile of a circular needle.

Straight needles, with one pointed and one capped end, are used exclusively for flat knitting and come in varied lengths and thicknesses.

Double-pointed needles come in sets of four or five needles and are used for knitting narrow tubes in the round—for projects such as socks, mittens, and the top of a hat.

Circular needles are pointed at both ends with a flexible coil in between and come in various lengths; they can be used for either circular or flat knitting. New circular needles usually have a stiff coil. Take the time to soften the coil by briefly dipping it in hot water before using.

Cable needles are short, sometimes curved, needles, with points at both ends, used to remove one or more stitches temporarily in order to perform a cable twist. I often use a toothpick or a double-pointed needle instead.

Accessories

Tapestry or yarn needles are hand-sewing needles used to work in yarn ends, embroider, and sew seams. Look for a big eye and a blunt tip.

Stitch holders allow you to set aside a portion of stitches while you work on another section. I like the kind that open on both ends.

Stitch markers are used to indicate where shaping or stitch patterns begin and end. Place the marker on the right hand needle when instructed. Slip it from the left to the right needle as you knit each row.

A row counter helps you keep track of how many rows you have knit—just turn the dial each time you complete a row. This is important information when working garment shaping or stitch patterns. Some prefer using old-fashioned pen-and-paper hatch marks or other notation systems. Any system is fine, as long as you stick to it and it makes sense to you.

A needle gauge allows you to identify the exact size of your needle and is especially helpful when you have a large selection of unmarked double-points and circulars.

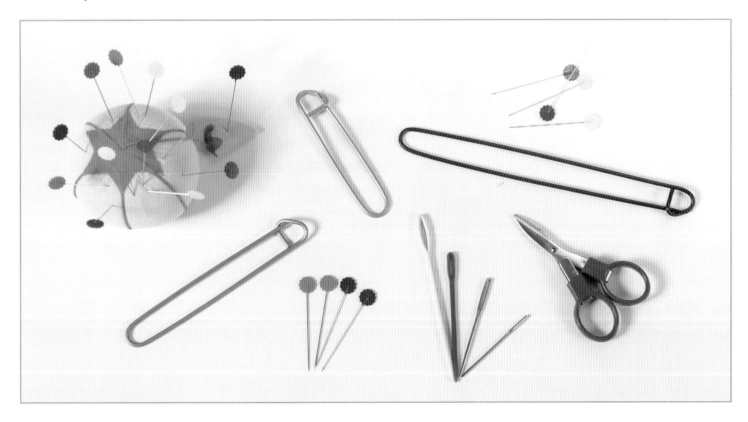

Rulers are used to measure gauge. Some needle gauges include rulers.

A tape measure is used to measure the length of your work when the directions give the length to work in inches rather than a specific number of rows.

Pins are handy for holding pieces of your work in position while you sew them together.

Needle cases are essential for organizing your needle collection. While there are a number of excellent ones commercially available, I prefer the charm of a homemade case.

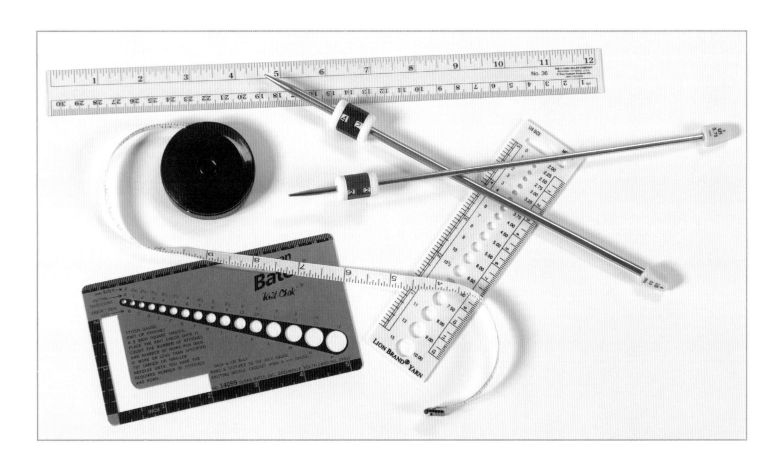

PART I · The Course

If you are new to knitting, I assure you that you *can* learn to knit from a book. As many others have before, you can teach yourself through reading books and experimentation. To get started, give yourself an undisturbed hour, some yarn and needles, a little patience, and you *will* knit. Read the instructions with yarn and needles in hand, step by step. Think of each step as a "dot" and follow the directions exactly as written, then practice connecting the "dots" in a continuous, fluid motion.

It is undeniably helpful to be able to watch someone else knit as you are learning. If you know someone who knits, ask them to cast on some stitches for you and to demonstrate the knit stitch. Get a little practice, then study the instructions and illustrations, and you'll be delighted by how quickly you grasp the basics. If you don't know any knitters yet, don't be discouraged: The Course in this book is designed to be self-taught. There are also good Internet resources that demonstrate basic knitting operations (Appendix D, page 141).

The essence of knitting can be reduced to just one stitch. That's all you need to focus on in the beginning—and breathing. When they work their first practice piece, new knitters often hold their breath for fear of messing up the stitches. Relax. The worst that can happen is that a few might slip off. Slip them back on any way you can and keep going. I call this "four-wheeling." The best advice I can give new knitters is don't be dismayed when you find a glitch in the row such as an extra wrap around the needle. "Drive" right over it, by just knitting it together with either neighboring stitch. If you suddenly have extra stitches, knit a couple of stitches together here and there to reduce the number. Your very first piece is expected to be odd-looking and funny shaped. Make it long enough and you can call it a scarf and keep it as a souvenir of your novice efforts.

The three basic operations of knitting are casting on (page 25), the knit stitch (page 26), and binding off (page 30). With these three skills, you can make scarves, blankets, pillows, hats—even a boxy sweater—with simple rectangles and squares. Part of the wonder of knitting is that anyone can learn how to knit in an evening, yet the variations are so limitless they keep the craft fascinating for a lifetime. The Underwater Afghan on page 55 is an example of what you can do with just the three basic operations and a palette of blues and greens.

Everyone knits differently and develops their own preferences and methods. While there are many right ways to knit, there is a conventional method that I have presented here in The Course. That said, even if your way differs, if it produces a wearable garment or useful object and you enjoy the process, then your way is the "right" way for you. Knit what you like and how you like. That said, remember that directions are written assuming that knitters work in the conventional method, so it is important to understand it.

Making a Slip Knot

Before you can knit, you must first *cast on*, or create a row of foundation stitches. The first stitch of this row is called a *slip knot*, which you may already know how to make. If so, use the method you're familiar with. Here's the classic method.

1. With thumbs about 2 inches apart, pinch the yarn with the cut, or *tail*, end in your right hand and the end connected to the ball, or *working yarn*, in your left hand. Leave a long tail if you plan to sew a seam later, otherwise a 4- to 6-inch tail will be sufficient for you to weave in later.

2. Bring your hands together, putting the right hand in front so that a loop forms. Pinch the loop with the left hand so the right hand is free to bring the tail to the back and behind the loop.

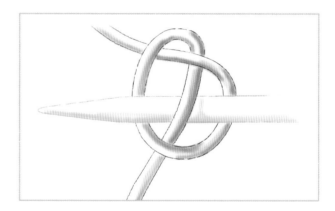

3. Lay the *loop* down and pick up the underlying strand with your needle and pull this new loop through the original loop. Pull the yarn strands gently to tighten the new loop around the needle. This loop is the first cast-on stitch.

The Right Way to Wrap the Yarn

"Forward under the needle, then up and back over the needle." After teaching hundreds of new knitters, I've noticed that nearly all share the inclination to wrap the yarn around the needle incorrectly, with the result that their stitches are backwards on the needle and thus easily twisted when the next row is worked. This curiosity has led me to conclude that the conventional way to knit (emphatically not the only way to knit) is actually counterintuitive for many people. Stop and check that you are actually wrapping the yarn around the needle in the direction of the arrow on the drawing. Practice makes the motion second nature.

Casting On

There are many ways to cast on and any method you happen to know is a good one. However, the *knit-on cast-on* is both easy to learn and produces excellent results. If you are left-handed, I urge you to find a way to work as explained here but use your left hand to wrap the yard. But if you prefer, you may switch hands.

1. Make a slip knot. Place your left hand over the needle with the slip knot and take the empty needle in your right hand. Put the right needle *in* through the first loop on the left needle by poking it from the front to the back (away from you), creating an X (drawing at left).

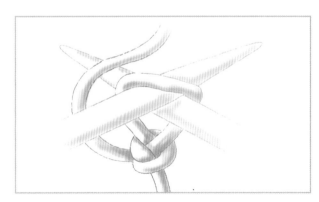

2. Pinch the left and right needles together so your right hand is free to grasp the working yarn and hold it below the right needle; wrap it forward, up, and *around* the right needle as shown above.

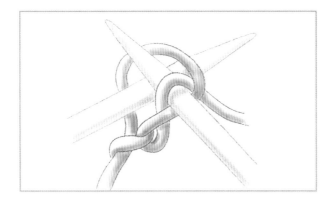

3. Lift your right elbow so your needles are at a right angle, draw the point of the right needle through the first loop, *under* the left needle, bringing a new loop through the first. Be sure to bring the yarn on the right needle through the stitch on the left needle to form a loop. This is the moment when a new stitch is born.

4. *Add* the new loop on your right needle to the left needle as shown in the bottom left drawing.

5. Remove the right needle from the loop. Adjust the loop by gently pulling on the working yarn so that it is neither too loose nor too tight. Congratulations! You have just knitted your first stitch and cast on a stitch. There are now two stitches on the left needle. Repeat, making each new stitch through the stitch last added to the left needle, for the desired number of stitches, about 10 to 12 to start.

The Knit Stitch

"Leave your brain out of it," I often tell my new students. What I mean is that until you feel fluent in knitting, which won't take long, don't worry too much about what you are doing. Knitting is a physical activity. It helps to literally talk yourself through the first few rows of knitting until you have programmed your *muscle memory*. As a new knitter, use this to your advantage by focusing on the four movements—*in, around, under,* and *off*—until you get the

hang of it. Since you have learned the knit-on cast-on, learning the knit stitch only requires learning one new step in place of the last cast-on step. The first three steps of the cast-on and knit stitch are identical, but the last step is *off* instead of *add*. As you work your first few knit stitches, try repeating the name of each movement aloud as you repeat each movement. The illustrations show a row of knitting in progress, with the completed stitches on the right needle. I really urge all left-handed knitters to keep their work in this orientation, pinching the needles together with the right hand and wrapping the yarn with the left. If you feel you must reverse your work to be comfortable, use a mirror to reverse the illustrations.

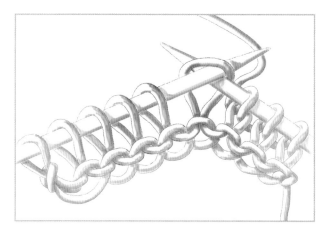

1. As you start to knit, have the working yarn *behind* your work. If it's not behind, move it there by passing it under the tip of the needle. Insert the right needle *in* through the first loop on the left needle by inserting it from the front to the back (away from you), creating an X, just as you did to cast on.

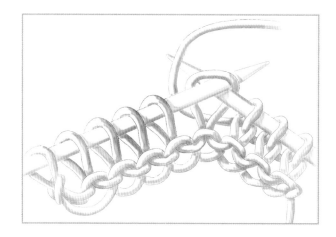

2. Pinch the left and right needles together so your right hand is free to grasp the working yarn and wrap it *around* (first forward under and then up and back over) the right needle.

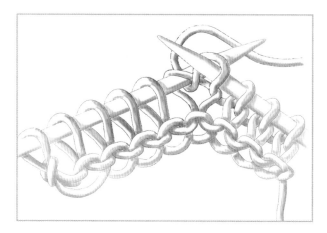

3. Lift your right elbow so your needles are at a right angle, draw the point of the right needle through the first loop on the left needle, *under* the left needle, bringing a new loop through.

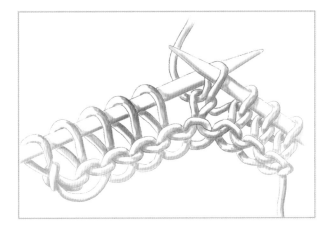

4. After you pull the new stitch through it, slide the old stitch *off* the left needle and let it drop. The dropped stitches form the first knit row under the right needle.

5. Continue to work each remaining stitch from the left needle, adding the new stitches to the right needle. When the row is completed, turn your work by transferring the right needle with all the stitches to your left hand and the now empty needle to your right hand. What was the back or wrong side of your work now faces you. Keeping the working yarn at the back of your work to knit, repeat steps 1 through 4 to knit the next row, turning your work at the end of each row as in step 5.

Smooth rhythm, even tension, and speed all come naturally with practice. Everyone knits a little differently and you will find a way that works for you. For

the first week try to knit a little every day—short frequent stints will help you retain and refine your skills.

The Purl Stitch

There is only one basic stitch in knitting but it has two sides: the knit side and the purl side. The purl stitch is really a knit stitch worked in reverse. The movements used to work are still *in, around, under* and *off.* These movements for the purl stitch take place in the front of your work instead of the back. The illustrations show a row of purling in progress, with the completed stitches on the right needle.

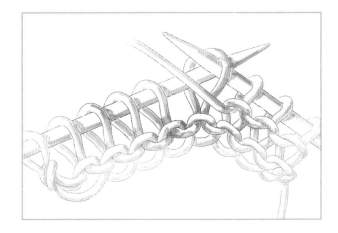

1. Insert the right needle *in* through the loop on the left needle from the back to the front (toward you). Before you wrap the yarn, be sure you have brought it forward under the tip of the needle so that it is in front of the work.

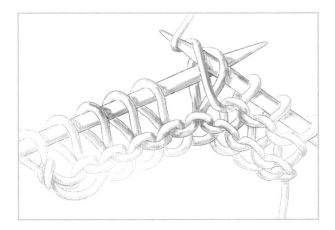

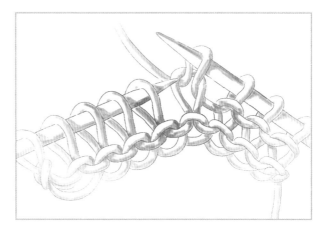

2. Wrap the yarn around the right needle, bringing it up and over to the back and then *around* the tip of the needle.

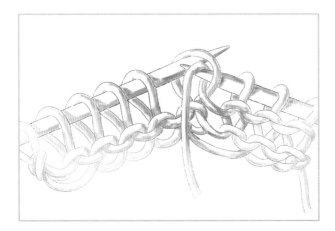

3. Use your left index finger to push the tip of the right needle through the loop on the left to the back, *under* the left needle.

4. Slide the left needle back out of the old stitch, dropping the old stitch off the needle.

Keeping the working yarn at the front, repeat steps 1 through 4 to purl across the row.

Knit and Purl

Basic Fabrics

Garter Stitch

Knitting every row creates a horizontally ridged pattern that looks the same on both sides. This easy to work texture has the virtue of lying flat, making it suitable for borders, as in the Flower Garden Blanket on page 70, or simple scarves. The Underwater Afghan on page 55 is composed entirely of this basic

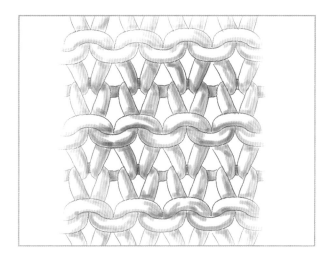

fabric. Although less commonly used, purling every row also creates garter stitch (above).

Stockinette Stitch

Stockinette stitch is what most people think of "regular" knitting, and it is worked by alternating one row of knit stitches with one row of purl stitches. The smooth knit side is usually used as the right side.

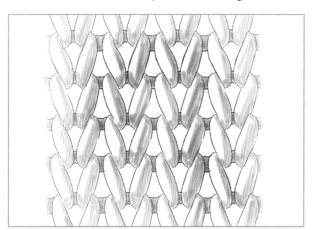

Reverse Stockinette Stitch

This pattern is identical to regular stockinette stitch, with alternating rows of knit and purl stitches. However, the bumpy side is used as the right side.

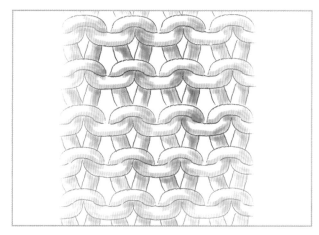

Binding Off

To finish your piece, you need to secure the stitches so they don't unravel. This is called *binding off*, or sometimes, *casting off*. One of the idiosyncrasies of knitting is that your bind-off may be too tight. To ensure a flexible finished edge, you can draw up a slightly longer loop as you work each stitch or simply use a larger needle than the one you are knitting with to work your bind-off row. Your goal is to have the bound-off edge correspond to knitted fabric itself, neither pulled in too tightly nor too loose and wavy.

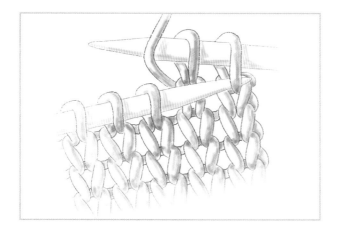

1. Knit two stitches. Draw the first stitch up and over the second stitch on the right needle, using either your fingers or the tip of the left needle.

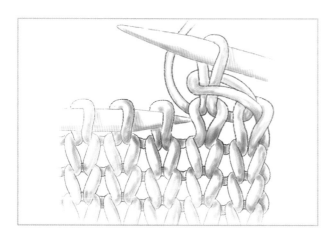

2. Drop the lifted stitch over the tip of the right needle. One stitch remains on the right needle.

3. Knit one more stitch.

Repeat steps 2 and 3 until you have one stitch left on your right needle. Take the needle out and loosen the loop. Cut the yarn and thread the cut end through the loop (as if the loop itself were a needle) and pull it tight to secure the last stitch.

More Basic Fabrics

Ribbing

Ribbing alternates knit and purl stitches in the same row. The most common variations are *1-by-1* (knit one stitch, purl one stitch) and *2-by-2 ribbing* (knit two, purl two). Because stockinette fabric curls quite noticeably, ribbing is used to stabilize and tighten the edges of hats, cuffs, necks, and hems. Ribbing is reversible and is a classic fabric for scarves.

To switch between knit and purl stitches in the same row, you must *move the yarn* back and forth as you change between knit and purl stitches, that is, when you *knit* the yarn must be in the *back* of your work and when you *purl* the yarn must be in the *front*. If you neglect to move the yarn back and forth under the needle, there will be lots of *yarn-over* holes resulting in many new stitches, hopelessly disturbing your pattern. I call this the knit-two purl-two waltz: knit two with the yarn at the back, pass the yarn under the tip of the right needle to the front, purl two with the yarn at the front, pass the yarn back under the needle to the back of your work: "Knit,

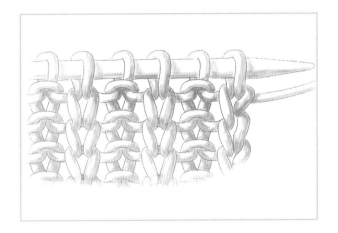

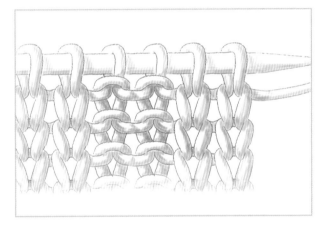

To bind off in ribbing or pattern

When directions say to bind off in ribbing or bind off in pattern, knit or purl each stitch as if you were working a normal pattern row, binding off each stitch as you go.

before you try twisting a cable, which is based on the vertical column structure of ribbing.

Cables

Twisting a cable is simply changing the order in which the cable stitches are worked. You do this by placing the first half of the cable stitches onto a "cable" needle to hold them out of the way while you work the second half, (below). You then slip the stitches from the cable needle back onto the left needle and work them, (opposite). Note that where you

knit, pass; purl, purl, pass." For 1-by-1 ribbing (top), you will need to pass the yarn after every stitch. When you work ribbing, be sure to work knit stitches over knit (smooth "vee") stitches and purl over purl (bumpy) stitches to keep the ribs aligned. Focus on the soothing rhythm of ribbing and your fingers will soon learn to "think" for you. The knee pads for crawlers on page 59 will give you practice with 2-by-2 ribbing. Ribbing is an important skill to practice

Looking at your work

Take a minute to examine your knit and purl stitches. Notice that the knit stitches form smooth "vees" on the side that faces you when you are knitting. When the knit stitch is still on the left needle, notice the left side (or leg) of the stitch loop is at the back of the needle (this is referred to as the back of the loop); the right side (or leg) of the loop is in front of the needle. When you insert the needle into the center of the loop to knit it, the loop turns slightly to form a flat stitch when it drops. If the loop faces the opposite direction on the needle, you will form a twisted stitch.

Notice that the purl stitches form a bumpy surface on the side facing you when you are purling. Think of the bump at the base of each purl stitch as a "pearl" to help you distinguish it from the "vee" side of the a knit stitch. Recognizing the smooth or bumpy side will help you to recognize which side of the work you are on.

Using a row counter helps too. In stockinette stitch, if row 1 is a knit row, then all odd-numbered rows are knit rows and all even-numbered rows are purl, or wrong-side rows. As you continue to learn new steps, stop to examine your work. Look at how the stitches are formed and how they relate to each other. This will help you follow stitch patterns more easily, because you will recognize what you are doing.

hold the cable needle determines the direction in which the cable twists. If you hold the cable needle stitches *in front* of the work as shown in the illustration, they will cross over the other half of the stitches when they are knitted, to make the cable twist to the *left*. If you hold the cable needle stitches *in back* of the work, the other cable stitches will cross over them to make the cable twist to the *right*. The Flower Garden Blanket on page 70 offers a lovely way to discover cables.

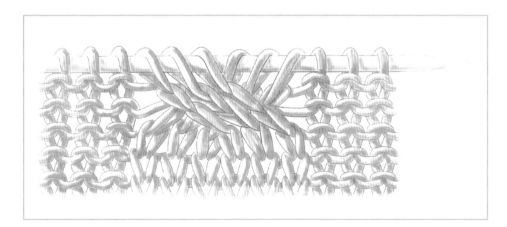

Lost and Found: Mystery Stitches

"Why does my knitting keep getting wider? is one of the most common questions among new knitters. The two most frequent bungles new knitters make create extra stitches, which cause the work to grow unexpectedly.

Mystery Stitch Culprit #1 occurs at the beginning of a row when the yarn is hanging over the tip of the needle to the back, making one stitch appear to be two. Before you start a new row, be sure the yarn is hanging below the needle.

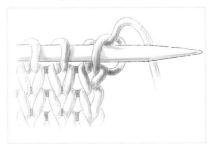

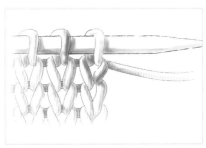

Culprit #2 happens when you put your knitting down in the middle of the row. When you pick up your knitting be sure the working yarn is coming from the last stitch on your right needle and hanging from the back if on a knit row and from the front if on a purl row. On a knit row, when the working yarn is in the front of

your work, knitting the next stitch will force the yarn up over the right needle, creating an extra stitch and a hole (below). This is

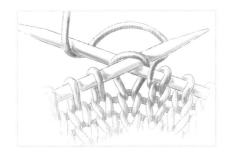

not always a mistake—it can also be a design element. When you do it as part of a pattern, it's called a *yarn over* and is one element of lace knitting. To avoid accidental holes, be sure the yarn is at the back of your work when knitting and in the front when purling. To switch it back and forth without adding an extra stitch, pass it under the tip of the needle.

The next irregularity occurs similarly to Culprit #2 except that when you pick up your work, you pick it up backward with the yarn hanging to the back from the last stitch on your left needle. Again, this is not always a mistake. In patterns it's

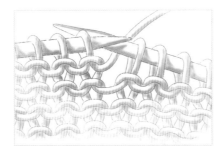

called a "short row" and has the effect of building up one side of your work higher than the other. Though it makes a hole in

your work unless you take preventative measures, working a short row does not create a new stitch. This technique is used in the Bunny Bonnet on page 104 and the Aran Hood on page 130, as instructed by "turn work in the middle of the row." If you stop in the middle of a row, be sure the needle with the yarn is in your right hand when you resume unless you intend to work short rows.

Your working yarn tells you where you are in the row. The stitch it is connected to is the last stitch that you knit. If the working yarn is not coming from the first stitch on the left needle when you begin a row (below), it means you have not finished the previous row. Put the full needle in your right hand and transfer, or slip, as

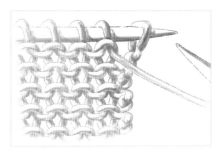

many not-knit stitches as you have to the left needle until the working yarn is available. You can now finish the row. If you stop in the middle of a row, be sure the needle with the working yarn is in your right hand when you resume (unless you intend to work short rows) and check that your yarn is coming from the stitch at the tip of the needle—you will avoid most common errors.

Seed Stitch

Seed stitch is another basic and nicely textured fabric that is similar to 1-by-1 ribbing. What distinguishes it from the vertical columns of ribbing is that you always "knit the purls and purl the knits," the exact opposite of "knit the knits and purl the purls." Although it can be worked on an even number of stitches by beginning alternate rows with knit and purl stitches, it is simplest to work on an odd number of stitches: Every row will then always begin with k1 followed by p1, k1, p1, k1 regardless of whether you are at the beginning of a right-side or a wrong-side row. Conversely, every row will always end with k1 too.

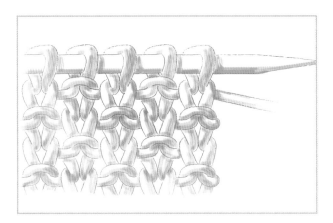

Adding a New Ball of Yarn

At some point you will need to connect another ball of yarn to complete a project. The easiest way is simply to tie the two ends together. Be sure to leave tails

of at least 6 inches so you can untie the knot later and work the tails into the stitches. Unless you are knitting in the round, join the new yarn at the edge.

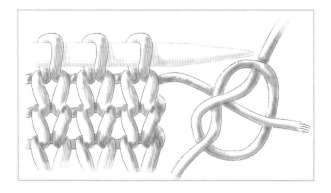

"How do I know if I have enough yarn to finish the row?" The *rule of three:* Your yarn needs to be about three times as long as the width of your work to finish the row. The exception to this rule occurs with binding off. To allow for the appropriately looser tension, your yarn should be four times as long as the width of your work.

To join yarn in circular knitting, work the first stitch of the round by knitting it with the old and new yarn held together. On the next row, when you

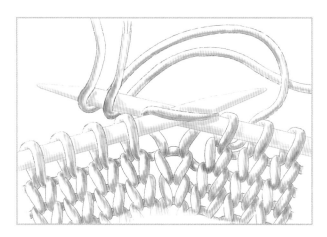

35

Adding color with stripes

Stripes are the easiest way to add color to your work, and they are an interesting way to learn how to count rows. Join the new color, leaving the old color hanging at the side without cutting it. Work your stripes in multiples of two rows, always picking up the working yarn from under the waiting yarn. Carrying the yarn this way makes a tidy candy-cane edge on scarves. A word of caution: If you cut the yarn each time you change colors, you will have a lot of ends to weave into the piece later. The Seaside Stripes Tee-Shirt on page 73 and Sun Hat on page 76 both use two-row stripes.

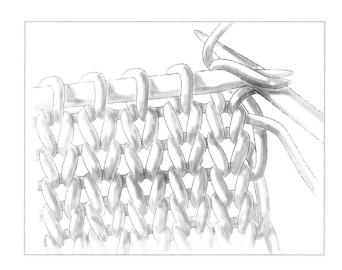

come to the two tails remember to knit this double-stranded stitch as one to avoid adding a stitch. This method helps to eliminate the jog when you change colors as you work rounds of circular knitting.

Occasionally you'll find a ready-made knot in your yarn. Manufactured knots are tough to undo and have no tails to work in. Cut these knots out and join the ends as for a new ball of yarn. While it's annoying to find such a knot near the end of the row, there are times when you may wish to avoid a mid-row join by unknitting, or "tinking", back to the beginning of the row (see page 43) to rejoin the yarn after cutting off the section with the offending knot. (You can save this scrap yarn for seaming.)

Shaping

Shaping is the process of subtracting or adding stitches from your work to make your fabric narrower or wider. For a hat, if you can start at the brim, you will decrease stitches at the top; for a sleeve, if you start at the cuff, you will increase to create more stitches as you work up the sleeve. As with most knitting operations, there are numerous ways to *decrease* and *increase,* but there's no need to learn them all now. You can usually substitute one method for another with only a slight change in appearance. Each has advantages and disadvantages that you can exploit as design opportunities. Following are several ways to do each. Binding off is also sometimes used to shape a piece.

Decreasing

The simplest way to *decrease* is to knit two stitches together. It is abbreviated as *dec* or *k2tog*. You can also purl two stitches together (p2tog). Both methods create a right-slanted stitch. When directions indicate k3tog, knit three stitches together. This decreases two stitches at the same time.

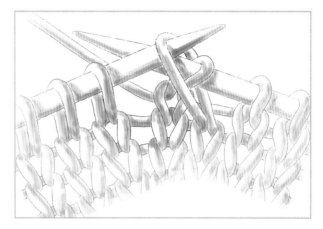

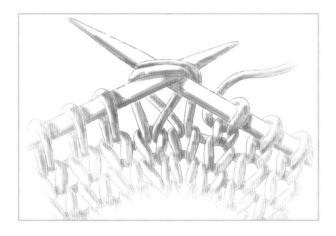

There are two methods to make a left-slanted decrease stitch. You start the first by *slipping a stitch*, transferring it from one needle to the other without knitting it. To slip a stitch, insert the right needle knitwise (from front to back), and withdraw the left needle, leaving the unworked stitch on the right needle. Knit the next stitch and then *pass the slipped stitch over* it (above right). Passing the slipped stitch over is exactly like binding off a stitch in the middle of a row and is abbreviated as *PSSO*. (You can also slip, or transfer a stitch back to the left needle from the right when needed.) This left slant decrease is usually abbreviated as *SKP*, or *sl1, k1, PSSO*.

A second, even simpler, way is the *SSK: slip, slip, knit* decrease. One at a time, slip two stitches to the right needle and then knit them together by inserting the left needle from the back towards you (from left to right) through the loops (below).

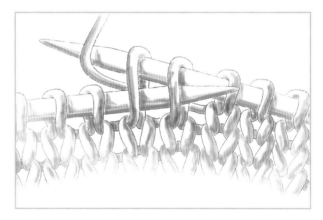

Increasing

There are two general methods of *increasing*: knitting twice into the same stitch and creating a new stitch between two stitches. The first, sometimes known as a *bar increase* because it makes a horizontal bar at the base of the new stitch, is made by first knitting into the front of the loop as usual. Then, instead of dropping the old stitch off the left needle, insert the right needle into the back of the loop of the same stitch and knit a second stitch (below). With the two new stitches on the right needle drop the old stitch off the left needle. It helps if you tilt your work forward so that you can see the back of the loop. Referring to the four steps of the knit stitch (in, around, under, and off), the formula for the bar increase is "first stitch in, around, under; second stitch in, around, under; and then off.

One way to create a stitch between two others, *the lifted increase*, is sometimes known as *make one* but I prefer "lifted" because that accurately describes what you are doing: lifting the ladder rung, the strand of yarn that runs horizontally between any two stitches. While there is no such thing as an entirely invisible increase, this is a less visible method of increasing than the bar increase.

To make a lifted increase, insert the left needle from the ladder rung (connecting strand) between the stitches on your right and left needles. Insert your right needle into the lifted loop, twisting the loop as shown in the bottom drawing, and knit a stitch. Take care, if you knit into the loop without twisting it, it will make a hole similar to a yarn over, which is explained next.

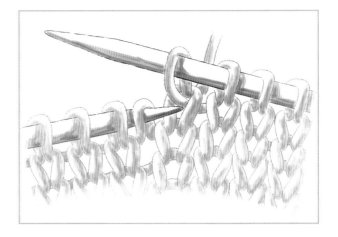

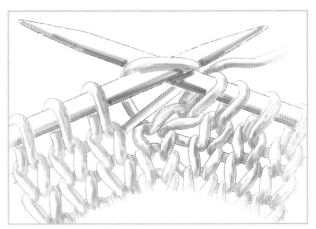

The *yarn over* also creates a stitch between two others. It is a simple loop made over the right needle. It forms a decorative hole or eyelet as on the Seeds and Vines Top-Down Cardigan (page 118). In lace patterns it is usually paired with decreases to maintain stitch count, as in the Feather and Fan Crib Blanket (page 111). To make a yarn over before a knit stitch, bring the yarn forward under the needle tip, then return the yarn to the back by wrapping it *over* the right needle to form the loop. Knit the next stitch to continue the row. On the following row, work the yarn-over loop as regular stitch.

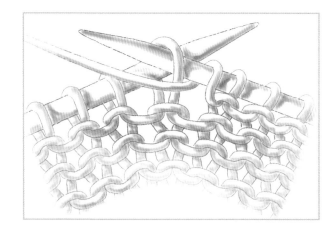

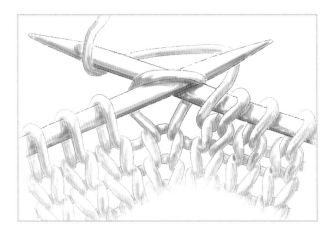

To make a yarn over just before a purl stitch, bring the yarn forward under the needle tip, wrap it back over the right needle to form the loop, and return it to rhe front of your work, passing it under the needle tip, ready to purl the next stitch (above right). Again, on the following row work the yarn-over loop as a regular stitch.

Circular Knitting

Knitting is usually done on two straight needles, working back and forth by turning the work 180 degrees at the end of every row. This is called flat knitting. It is also possible to knit in a circle, making a seamless tube on a flexible circular needle. The circular needle allows you to join the beginning and the end of the row, with the stitches spread out along the length of the wire between the needle points at each end. Be careful not to twist your cast-on row around the needle when joining the first round: The cast-on edge is a thin ridge that wants to twirl in a spiral around your needle. To avoid this notorious bungle, check that your stitches are all hanging straight down with the cast-on edge at the bottom (the stitches at the right-hand needle tip will rotate as you knit the join). Before you join, mark the beginning of the round by placing a marker on the right-hand needle tip (after the last stitch cast on); then knit the first stitch of the next round (the first stitch cast on). Note that a row is called a *round* when the work is joined on a circular needle. On subsequent rounds, slip the marker from the left-hand needle tip to the right-hand needle tip as you would in flat knitting. As you knit, the stitches will slide from the rigid tips onto the wire portion of the needle. This is no cause for alarm since the stitches are at no risk, and will slide back onto the thicker pointed ends when needed.

Note that when you are working flat, garter stitch is formed when you knit every row. You may be surprised to find that when working in the round, knitting every row produces stockinette fabric rather than garter stitch. This is because you are always facing the outside, or right side of your work. Thus, garter stitch is formed on a circular needle by alternating one round of knit stitches with one round of the purl stitches.

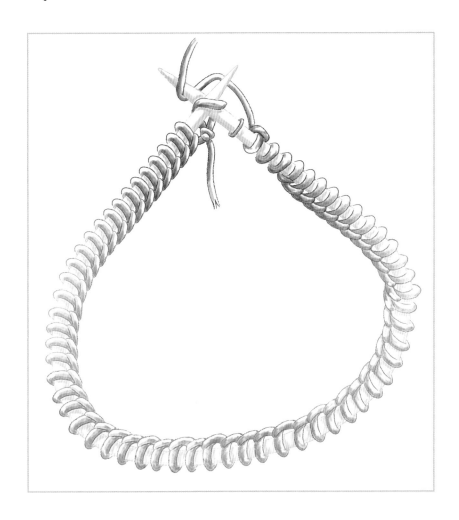

Refining Your Style

As you add more complicated maneuvers to your repertoire, work close to the tips of your needles. When the stitches are on the thick part of the needle there is less room to insert the right needle. By keeping your stitches close to the points, you create more room to maneuver. However, this is a little precarious because stitches can fall off the needles. Prevent stitches from falling by using the tips of your index fingers to keep them in place. In time, your fingers will automatically feed the stitches up the left needle and down the right needle.

I-Cords

I-Cords are another form of circular knitting based on the four-stitch knitting spools that children use to make those long snakes that can be coiled into potholders, mats, rugs, etc. To make I-cord, use two double-pointed needles. Cast on three stitches. Knit, and instead of turning your work at the end of every row, slide the stitches to the other end of the right-hand needle and transfer it to your left hand. When you make the first stitch of the next row, the working yarn is forced across the back of the work as shown at right. After you've knit several rows, pull down on the tube; the extra yarn automatically redistributes so that you have a perfect tube. I-cords can be executed on anywhere from two to six stitches. They can also be applied as an attached edging (see Edgings, on page 50).

Fixing Mistakes

Nobody's perfect: Mistakes happen to everyone, even the most experienced knitters. Take a deep breath; relax. There are methods to fix even the most cumbersome errors.

Dropped Stitches

Here is an exercise to overcome forever your fear of dropped stitches. With practice yarn, cast on 16 to 20 stitches. Work in stockinette stitch for two to three inches. With the right side facing you, knit to the middle of the row. Take a deep breath and slide a stitch off a needle. Stretch your work sideways so that the stitch runs down several rows. You will see a *ladder* between the stitches. No matter how many rows down, place the lost stitch onto the right needle, placing the left strand of the loop in front. Taking the ladder rungs in order, place the one at the bottom over the right needle and then pull the lost stitch over the rung and off the needle. This is just like binding off or PSSO. Continue re-knitting the rungs until you reach the top. Then place the stitch back on the left needle with the right strand of the loop in front. (You can also use a crochet hook to chain up the ladder.)

While you can re-purl stitches by placing the ladder rung in front of the dropped stitch, it is easier to

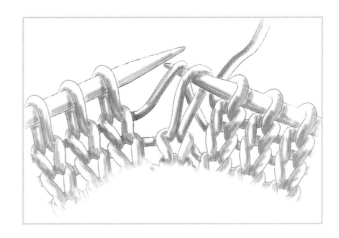

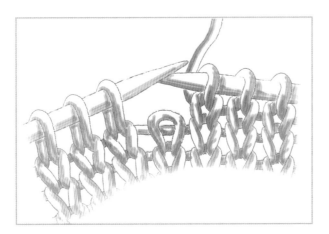

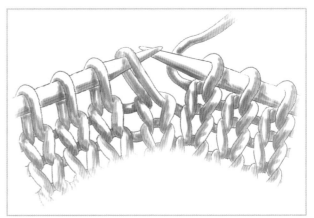

correct dropped stitches from the knit side—so just turn your work around so the knit side faces you. Garter stitch is a little more complicated because you must be able to distinguish the knits from the purls in order to know how the next rung should be worked (see "Looking at your work," page 33). It takes patience and practice to develop familiarity with the structure of knitting. Once you do, you will be able to correct anything.

Fallen Stitches

At some point or other, your stitches will fall off the needle. This is not a big deal, but you want to put them back on the needle right away to prevent your work from unraveling. If lots of stitches fall off the needle, it is much easier to put a them back on if you use a needle that is much thinner than the one you are knitting with. On the next row you can knit them back onto the correct size needle. Get in the habit of pushing your work down the needle before turning to prevent fallen stitches at the end of the row.

Tinking

If you discover that you have a twisted stitch or an extra stitch only a row or two back, you can literally rewind, or un-knit your knitting, sometimes known as *tinking* ("tink" is "knit" backwards). Insert the left needle into the stitch below the last stitch on the right needle and lift it, at the same time pull back on

the right needle so that the upper stitch slides off the right needle. It helps if you hold the yarn coming from the left as illustrated so that the stitch you are inserting the left needle into is pulled open.

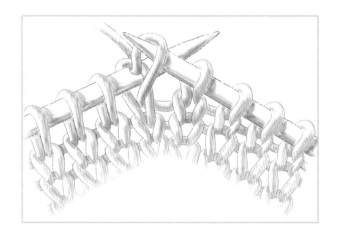

Ripping Out Stitches

For errors several rows down, it's fastest to take your work off the needles and pull the yarn so the stitches unravel. Here are two tips to make it easier to put your work back on the needles: First, rip down to one row above the error. You can then pull out and put the stitches back on the needle one by one and not worry about dropped stitches. Second, use a needle several sizes smaller so it slides easily through the loops. When you work the next row, you can correct any strange stitches. Remember that each stitch is a loop. Each loop has two legs; the right leg should be in front of the needle unless your directions specify otherwise. When you put a dropped stitch back on the needle remember "right is front," and you will avoid twisted stitches.

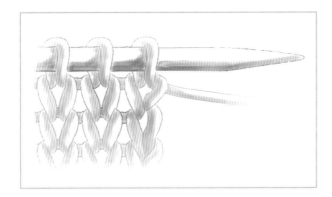

The Gauge Swatch

Measuring gauge accurately is the only way to ensure that your project will be the intended size. Gauge indicates how many stitches are in one inch of a given stitch pattern. It is the product of three factors: the size of the needle, the thickness of the yarn, and you. Everyone knits differently which is why you must *always* do a test-sample for each project using the yarn and needle size recommended in the directions. The suggested needle size to obtain the correct gauge is just that—a suggestion. You may need a larger or a smaller needle depending on the tension of your stitches. If your stitches are too tight and you have more stitches per inch than the directions call for, use a larger needle. If your stitches are too loose (fewer stitches per inch), use a smaller needle. You need to find the size needles that will give *you* the stated gauge or your work will not be the expected size.

Because knitted fabric has so much elasticity, understanding the way the fabric behaves is crucial to measuring accurately. Stockinette fabric has a tendency to spread out and become wider. Lace looks best when dramatically stretched and so takes fewer stitches to equal one inch. Ribbing and cable stitches pull together and thus require comparatively more stitches per inch.

Because stitch patterns behave differently, to reduce distortion many instructions direct you to test gauge over stockinette stitch as a baseline. Always cast on enough stitches for at least 4 inches in width and work at least 2 inches before taking your swatch off the needles to measure. For the most accurate results, bind off your four-inch patch loosely and take the time to block lightly. Gently spread the fabric to its full natural width without stretching it; measure it. Divide the total number of stitches by the measured width of your swatch to find the number of stitches per inch. As with any average, the larger your sample the more accurate your calculations will be. If the pattern stitch used for the project is new to you, make another swatch using the pattern stitch. It's a good way to see if you really like the pattern before you begin the project.

The time, love, energy, and money you invest in every project make it well worth your while to take the time to test your materials before casting on. If you're impatient and jump right in, be forewarned that your results may be too big or too small and your yarn supply incorrect.

A Note on Different Styles of Knitting

American- and English-style knitters hold the working yarn in the right hand (top right). Continental knitters hold the yarn in the left hand (bottom right). Consequently, left-handers and crocheters may prefer the Continental style.

No matter which hand you use, there are many individual variations on how to hold the yarn. The traditional method is to thread the yarn over and under the fingers on the right hand, letting it glide through your fingers as you knit. Since I am self-taught, I've developed an efficient method of pinching the yarn lightly between my thumb and forefinger, using a tiny whole-wrist motion to wrap. Some South American knitters use a variation on the continental method with the yarn wrapped around the neck so it feeds from behind.

The main advantage of continental knitting is that by threading the yarn through the left fingers one can pick up the yarn by "wrapping" the right needle over the yarn held taut by the left hand, thereby streamlining the process.

You might like to learn both ways so you can knit color patterns most efficiently: Hold one color in the right hand and the other color in the left and then work the American (right) and Continental (left) styles respectively. Indeed, two-color knitting is ideal for learning a second method: focus on the color pattern and your hands will figure out what to do. You can watch how other people knit to pick up subtle nuances as you continue to refine your technique.

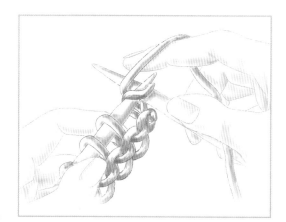

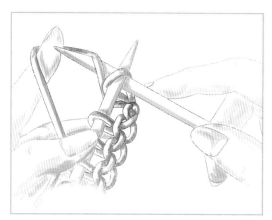

The Art of Finishing

Finishing distinguishes the transformation of yarn into attractively detailed garments. The only way to learn and competently apply finishing techniques is to practice patiently on swatches until you are confident. Experience is your best teacher. Together with common sense, it will guide you in finding the most elegant finishing solutions. Trust your instincts. Do your best and remember that even the experienced knitters delight in learning new tricks. If your first efforts aren't as perfect as you like, be inspired by the charm of having figured out your own unique way of putting something together. There is no right or wrong way, just your own way.

The art of knitting can be separated into two distinct phases: (a) that of constructing the fabric and

45

(b) that of constructing the garment. So far, this Course has focused primarily on the first part, that of making fabric. The second part—blocking, joining seams, and adding the finishing touches—often intimidates beginners. Be assured that any method you devise to join two pieces of fabric by hand with any sort of stitches qualifies both functionally and artistically as a "seam." You may also wish to learn the two versatile, conventional methods presented below.

You might be surprised to learn you love sewing seams. You might also be surprised to learn that for many projects I recommend you budget 50% of the time that you spend on the knitting (constructing the fabric), for the construction of the garment (sewing the seams and adding finishing touches). That is, if you spend 40 hours knitting the pieces, budget 20 hours for finishing. If you finish in 12-15 hours, you'll be thrilled to be ahead of schedule. The point is that finishing always takes longer than you expect. Avoid disappointing last-minute rushes by allotting plenty of time for finishing as prescribed above.

You can learn how to join seams with ease and confidence with a little practice. The way to polish your skills is first to be very patient, and then very disciplined. It takes intense focus to learn needle arts from illustrations and descriptions alone. If possible, have someone demonstrate each technique before or while studying the text. Plain worsted or bulky weight yarn is best for practice.

Blocking

Blocking allows you to refine the shape of the pieces of your project or garment before assembling them, straightening up any uneven edges or stitches in the process. Always check the yarn label for the manufacturer's blocking directions. Some synthetics require no blocking and some may actually be damaged by applying heat or steam.

For yarns that can be blocked, such as wool yarns, roll the pieces in a damp towel and leave them rolled up overnight to absorb some moisture from the towel. Place a dry towel on a flat surface over a layer of newspapers. Then lay the damp pieces out flat on the dry towel, patting them into the desired measurements, making sure the edges are straight and any contoured shaping, as for the neckline or armhole, is smooth. Leave the pieces undisturbed to air-dry completely before seaming.

Seams

There are two kinds of seams used in this book. The *flat seam* which is versatile and easy to learn, is used in many of the projects, including the Swing Coat on page 64 and the Underwater Afghan on page 55. The *mattress stitch seam* is invisible from the outside, but it makes a thick seam because it incorporates a whole stitch at the edge of each piece of fabric. It is usually used to seam stockinette fabric and is used to sew the sleeves of the Round-Yoke Sacque on page 122. Even though invisible, because of the thickness of this seam, I avoid it in garments knit on a gauge of 4 or fewer stitches to the inch.

The Flat Seam

Garter stitch is ideal for practicing flat seams because the "ridge and trough" structure of garter stitch forms easy-to-see bumps that you can use to literally zip up your seams. I call this the *bump to bump to bump* method. With right sides facing you, bring your needle up, always pointing in the same direction, parallel to the seam, passing it through a "bump" on each side alternately. The flat seam preserves the maximum width of your fabric.

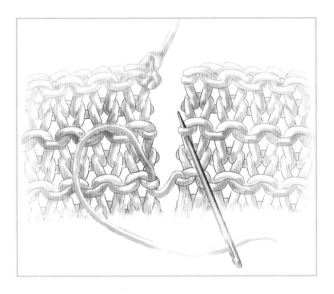

The Mattress Stitch Seam

This seam is worked from the right side so you can see the end result as you are sewing.

1. Insert the needle into the space one stitch in from the edge and pick up one ladder rung (the strand between the first and second stitches).

2. Pick up one ladder rung from the edge of the other piece to be joined, inserting the needle into the space corresponding to the one where you brought the needle out on the other side.

3. Repeat step two, working back and forth from side to side.

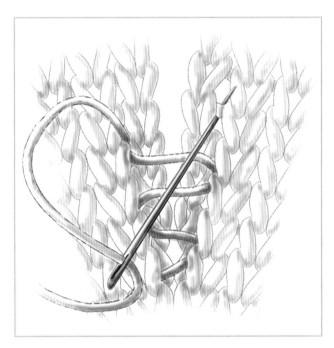

When working at more than 3 stitches to the inch, it is much faster to pick up the ladder rungs two by two. Every inch or so, adjust the tension of the seam by pulling the yarn gently but firmly.

The Three-Needle Bind Off

The *three-needle bind off* is included here with seaming methods because it actually eliminates sewing a seam. It is used to join the shoulders on the Middlebury V-Neck Pullover on page 97 and the Hibiscus Hooded Zip Jacket on page 90. Rather than binding off each piece separately and then seaming, join shoulders perfectly with the three-needle bind off.

If you haven't used circular needles for both knitting and holding stitches, then you will need to prepare by slipping the stitches of each edge to be bound off from its stitch holder onto a separate double-pointed needle, being careful not to twist the stitches (see the drawing on page 44).

With right sides together, hold both pieces in your left hand. Hold a third needle in your right hand. Knit the first stitches on each left needle together as one by inserting the right needle through both and bringing the new stitch through them. Repeat (shown below). Continue as for regular binding off as shown above right.

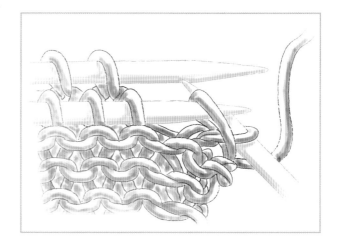

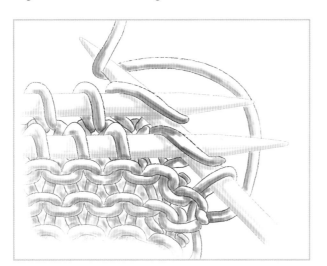

Picking Up Stitches

Picking up stitches allows you to create a new row of stitches along an existing edge without casting on. It is often used to add a border, such as a neckband, to a finished piece. Along with seams, with practice, this technique will give your garments a professional finish. It is very similar to knitting:

Insert the right needle through a stitch on a holder or one stitch down from the edge, wrap the yarn around the needle and pull the new stitch through. To pick up with the grain be sure to pick up each stitch from the middle of the "vee," not the "hat" (below and top right).

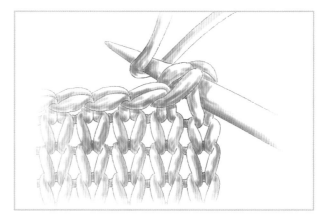

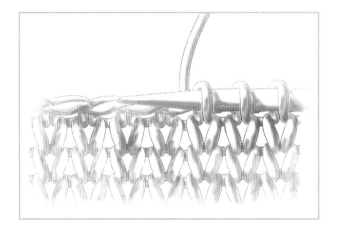

Picking up stitches along the side of knitting is trickier than picking them up at a bound-off end. You can practice this technique by picking up stitches along a garter stitch edge, one stitch in each trough between ridges. Picking up along the edge on stockinette fabric requires a little fiddling: One stitch for every row is too many, one for every other row too few. Pick up two stitches for three rows or three stitches for four rows or as needed to make a smooth edge with stitches evenly distributed.

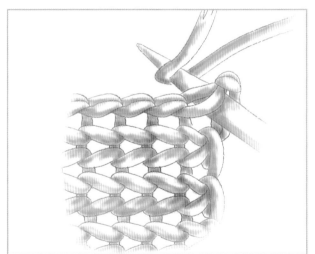

Weaving in Tails

Weave yarn tails into the work so there are no loose ends poking out anywhere. Thread each tail onto a yarn needle and, along the edge or interior, just skim the wrong side of the fabric as you weave.

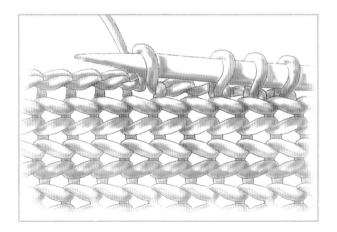

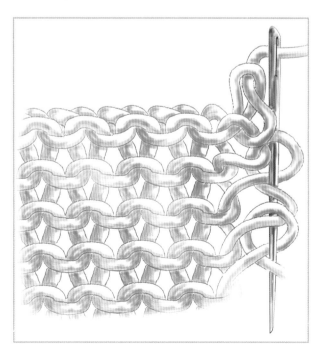

49

By virtue of its fuzziness and inherent stick-to-itself-ness, wool is by far the most cooperative fiber to work with. For that reason, weave in tails not needed for seaming before blocking, since blocking has a natural tendency to make the worked in ends stay in place. Cotton, with little stick-to-itself-ness, sometimes needs to be hand sewn with needle and thread to keep the ends from perpetually popping out. Such are the idiosyncrasies of knitting. When possible, weave tails into the fabric along an edge. Weave each tail in for at least 1½-2 inches before trimming it. On garter stitch fabric, pick up diagonally by picking up one stitch from a "ridge" alternated by one stitch from a "trough."

Buttonholes

There are two general methods of making horizontal buttonholes. The first simply uses a yarn over followed by knitting two stitches together. On most gauges, the yarn over increase creates a hole sufficient

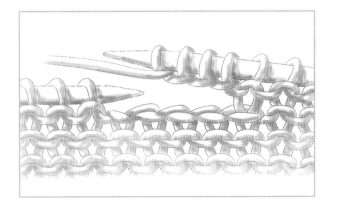

for a ⅜"- to ⅝"-diameter button. This type of buttonhole is used in the sundresses on pages 79 and 82.

The second is a two-row method. First, bind off two, three, or even four stitches (for a large button) in the appropriate place. On the second row, cast on, using the knitted-on method, (page 25), in the gap to restore your stitch count and close the buttonhole.

Zippers

Lay out the two knit pieces, butting the edges where the zipper is to go. Using sewing thread in a contrasting color, baste the pieces together with long diagonal stitches; keep the pieces flat. This ensures that they will meet exactly when zipped up, neither gaping nor overlapping. Then, using 1-inch stitches and starting at the hem, baste the zipper to the inside (make sure the zipper pull faces the knitting). The zipper is rigid and your work is elastic, so be sure not to stretch the fabric or the zipper will buckle. Evaluate the results of your basting honestly. If necessary, take it out and re-do. When you are confident the zipper is basted in correctly, stitch it in place by hand or machine, using sewing thread. Remove the basting thread and congratulate yourself on a job well done.

Edgings

Edgings are another kind of finishing that can be worked either at a 90-degree angle to your work or separately and applied later, as with the Victorian Eyelet Sundress on page 82. To work at a 90-degree angle, as at the back neck of the Middlebury V-Neck Pullover on page 97, cast on the required number of stitches for the edging. On each right side row, knit the last stitch of edging together with the next body stitch on left needle. Turn, and do not knit a body stitch and an edge stitch together on the wrong side. Work until all the body stitches have been incorporated.

An I-cord trim (see page 41) can be added to an edge by knitting the last stitch of every I-cord row together with one stitch picked up from the edge. The best way to practice this is to work it on a swatch in a contrasting color.

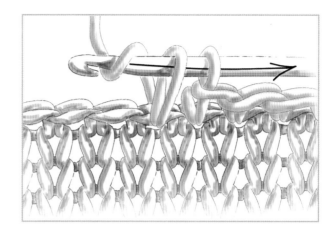

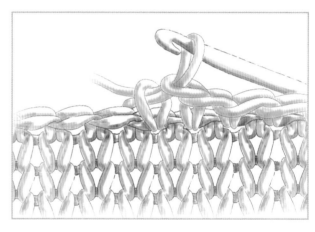

Crochet

Crochet and knitting are intimately related, since both are formed by interconnected loops. Crochet is created using a single hook instead of needles, and only the active stitch is on the hook. Because crochet

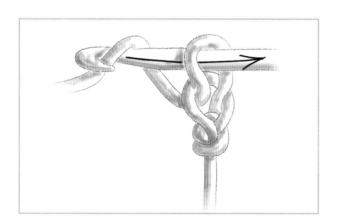

is a freer form of needlework than knitting, it is an easy and effective way to finish knitted edges.

Here are the basics to get you started: At left, chain stitch for button loops (begin with a slip knot just as for knitting). Above, single crochet worked onto an existing edge for trim.

Embroidery

If you've never embroidered before, practice with embroidery thread on fabric first. When working on a knitted fabric, be sure you don't pull the thread too tightly. A looser tension will make your stitches pop out more.

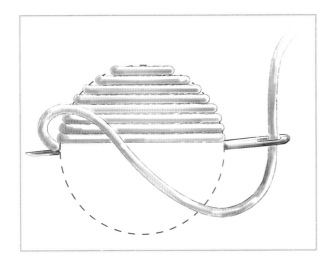

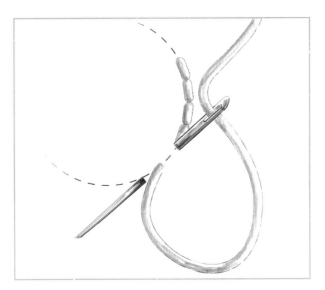

The Cuddly Bunny on page 108 features embroidery stitches for the facial features. Illustrated are satin stitch and backstitch.

Final Blocking

Blocking can be as simple as your regular washing procedure. Many projects require little if any traditional blocking.

However, careful blocking is crucial to the success of certain kinds of seamless garments, like the Swing Coat (page 64) and Origami Kimono (page 85). The simple construction provides no internal structure, so the fabric is likely to stretch out of shape when wet. To streamline future washings, cut a paper pattern according to the schematics given with the directions.

Care Instructions

Dry-cleaning is harsh on your hand-knits, expensive, and unnecessary. Hand-washing is best: Using gentle soap in cool water, soak the garment for 5 to 10 minutes. Agitate lightly. Avoid wringing out the water, roll in towels instead. Protect your floor or table from moisture damage with a flattened cardboard box covered with towels; lay the knitting on top to dry. Many synthetics can be machine-washed and dried. Check the label for the manufacturer's directions.

Gifts

When presenting a hand-knitted gift, include a hang tag with care instructions. Also include a yard of the yarn for possible repairs. My sweaters and blankets all come with a lifetime warranty, and do occasionally return for mending.

Reading a Knitting Pattern

There are just a few more things you need to learn before you embark on your first real project. To follow the directions for a knitting project, you need to understand them; here are some basics to help you succeed in that.

Pattern Repeats

Before embarking on complex pattern designs you must understand how *pattern repeats* function and how to use stitch markers. *Repeat* means "the number of stitches it takes to do the pattern once." A 2-by-2 rib is a repeat of four stitches; a 1-by-1 rib is a repeat of two. The repeat is usually expressed as "a multiple of" a specified number of stitches, and for every size given in the project directions, the cast-on stitches or a set-up row before you begin the pattern will be equal to this multiple. Some pattern repeats are stated as "a multiple of plus" (for a few extras stitches added to make the pattern begin and end symmetri-

cally). A multiple of 10 stitches plus 1 means the cast-on row will have 11, 21, 31, etc. stitches. Placing a stitch marker between repeats will aid in keeping track of where each repeat begins and ends. As you work a row with markers, slip the marker from the left to the right needle when you come to it. You can also place a marker every 10 or 20 stitches as you cast on to make counting easier. When you are familiar with the pattern, you can remove the markers.

Written Directions

Written directions often use abbreviations and special terms to save space and let the knitter understand at a glance, without too much reading. Many of the abbreviations are easy to remember: *k* means knit, *p* means purl, *inc* means increase, and so on. If you find unfamiliar abbreviations or terms in the directions, check Appendix A on pages 137-138.

Schematic Drawings

Schematic drawings give the exact dimensions of each part of each garment, after blocking. Schematic drawings of the garments in this book are given with the project instructions. They function as an overview and allow you to see the outline of your garment and the size of each part, facilitating necessary alterations. If your knitting is very different from the schematics, double-check your gauge. Use the schematics as a blocking guide.

PART 2

The Projects

Underwater Afghan

Stripes of varying hues of blue and green are soothing and reminiscent of the way light refracts through reedy lake water. Though exceedingly simple to work, the combined effect is of a complex cubist painting. You can reproduce the afghan exactly as pictured, or knit your own version by randomly varying the width but keeping a uniform length for each strip.

For a special shower gift, enlist several other knitters in your family to each knit a strip. Wind off small balls of each color to make 5 individual palettes, roughly equal in size. The knitting is simple enough to include young and new knitters. If five families participate, each can make a family strip incorporating all available knitters. Some may wish to knit only a few stitches while others will zoom along. Everyone can contribute without feeling pressured to do more than they wish. Some people will knit tightly and others loosely, resulting in strips of varying width. This is not a problem! The wavy lines will reiterate the watery theme. To assemble the strips, lay them out like puzzle pieces and see where the convex and concave parts fit best, rearranging as you like. Keep in mind that flat seaming will even out the gaps and overlaps, creating a cohesive, though not necessarily square, fabric.

Experiment with texture patterns if you want a more challenging project. For a full-sized afghan, make wider strips to cut down on seaming and weaving in the tails of yarn. If you want lots of small color units, consider backing your afghan with fabric to avoid weaving in tails altogether. Though demanding, I enjoy taking the time to finish the back so the afghan is truly reversible. This afghan contains 98 yarn tails, so allow several hours for finishing.

Underwater Afghan

Size

About 28" by 30" square

Materials

Needles: 24"-long circular needle size 9 (5.5mm), or size needed to obtain correct gauge; needle size 10½ (6.5mm) for binding off (optional)

Yarn: Cascade Yarns, 1 skein of each of the following:

A	Med. Green	220	#9430	Highland Green
B	Dk. Teal Blue	220	#4009	Aporto
C	Lt. Blue	220	#9452	Summer Sky Heather
D	Med. Blue	220	#9456	Sapphire Heather
E	Lt. Blue	220	#9325	West Point Blue Heather
F	Med. Multi Green	220 Quatro	#9435	Jamaica
G	Med. Blue	220 Tweed	#9414	Ocean Tweed

Gauge

18 sts = 4" in stockinette stitch

AFGHAN

Make five strips, each 200 rows in length: Leaving an 18" yarn tail, cast on stitches as indicated in the table for each strip. Work in garter st (knit every row) changing colors as listed. Mark one side of your work with a safety pin to indicate the RS of work. When you change colors, always start the first row of the new color with the marked RS facing you, to keep a neat line between the colors. When all 200 rows are completed, bind off sts loosely, with a larger needed if needed. If you are not using a row counter, remember that 200 rows equals 100 garter stitch "ridges."

Strip #1:
Cast on 17 sts.

Col.	Number of rows	Number of ridges
A	44	22
B	14	7
C	26	13
D	22	11
E	10	5
F	34	17
G	22	11
A	6	3
B	22	11

Strip #2:
Cast on 21 sts.

D	38	19
E	60	30
B	12	6
G	16	8
F	12	6
A	20	10
C	8	4
F	34	17

Strip #3:
Cast on 27 sts.

G	48	24
C	52	26
A	12	6
F	28	14
B	36	18
E	24	12

Strip #4:
Cast on 15 sts.

Col.	Number of rows	Number of ridges
C	42	21
A	10	5
B	22	11
E	30	15
D	18	9
A	34	17
G	44	22

Strip #5:
Cast on 23 sts.

F	34	17
D	54	27
B	14	7
G	30	15
E	10	5
C	38	19
A	20	10

Note: Cast-on edges are at top of afghan in photo.

Finishing

Arrange strips following diagram and photo for placement. Sew flat seams.

Block lightly, if desired.

Borders: With first color (see list below), pick up 100 stitches evenly spaced along one side edge. If you counted your rows accurately, this works out to exactly one stitch in each garter stitch "trough." (Don't worry if you need to fudge a little.) Inc 1 stitch at the beg of every row to form miter, knit 3 rows of first color and 4 rows each of second and third colors. Bind off loosely. Repeat on the opposite edge. Repeat on each end, picking up about 94 sts on each.

Use colors listed for each border (oriented as in photo).

Top border: C, F, E.

Left border: A, G, B.

Bottom border: E, F, C.

Right border: B, G, D.

Sew short seams where mitered corners of borders meet. Weave in yarn tails.

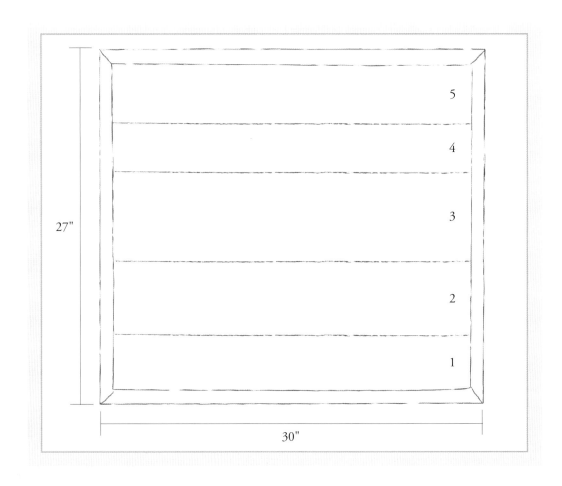

Safety Orange Knee Pads

Safety Orange Knee Pads
(See next page for instructions)

These cushy knee pads take only a few hours to knit and will give you practice knitting and purling in the same row by working 2-by-2 ribbing. The long rectangle folds in half to make a double-thick fabric for extra padding. The one-stitch garter stitch border takes a little extra care to work correctly on the wrong sides, but it dramatically simplifies seaming; just remember to knit the first and last stitches of every row.

If you're a new knitter, notice the difference between your first and second pads and admire the progress you've made. Don't fret if they're not perfect, they will be much used and loved even if only for a few weeks of energetic crawling. Once outgrown, recycle into adult wrist warmers as a souvenir.

Materials

Needles: 1 pair of straight needles size 10½ (6.5mm), or the size needed to obtain the correct gauge.
Yarn: Cascade Yarns, 1 skein Pastaza #1050 (Burnt Orange), or 2 skeins Cotton Rich #3611 (Tomato)

To make **adult-sized leg warmers** cast on about half again the number of stitches (or 52 stitches) and work for desired length, using about 100 grams of yarn per warmer.

Gauge

14 sts = 4" in stockinette stitch

KNEE PADS

Make two.
Leaving an 18" tail, cast on 34 sts.
Row 1: *K2, p2; rep from *, end k2.
Row 2: K1, p1, *k2, p2; rep from*, end last rep with p1, k1.
Repeat rows 1 and 2 for pattern. Continue until work measures 8 inches. Bind off.

Finishing

Fold each piece in half lengthwise. Sew long edges together with flat seams. Weave in yarn tails.
Block lightly, if desired.

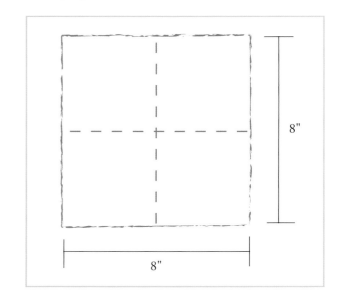

Apple Picker's Basket-Weave Poncho

Quick to throw on over a sweater on crisp autumn days, this poncho (shown on the following page) is also quick to knit. It can be worn with the vee at the front or to the side to make a more cape-like poncho.

The stitch is not a true basket-weave, but engrossing to work nonetheless. The simple texture is formed with 3 by 3 ribbing that shifts over 3 stitches every 4 rows. The ribbing also features garter stitch rather than reverse stockinette. That means you knit across the right side rows and only work the pattern on wrong-side rows.

Sizes

3-6 months (6-12 months, 12-18 months)

Materials

Needles: 16"-long circular needle size 10½ (6.5 mm), or size needed to obtain correct gauge

Yarn: Cascade Yarns, 2 (2, 3) skeins Pastaza #1008 (Periwinkle), or #1083 (Aberdeen Heather)

Gauge

14 sts = 4" in stockinette stitch

PONCHO

Make two pieces.

Leaving a 24" tail, cast on 33 (39, 45) sts.

Rows 1 through 5: Knit.

Rows 6 and 8 (WS): *K3, p3*; rep from * to *, end k3.

Rows 7, 9, 11: Knit.

Rows 10 and 12: K3, *k3, p3*; rep from * to *, end k6.

Rows 13-60: Repeat rows 5 through 12 for 6 more times.

Rows 61-64: Repeat rows 5 through 8.

Rows 65-68: Knit.

Bind off somewhat tightly.

For an **adult poncho**, cast on enough stitches for each piece to measure 20" to 22" wide, and bind off when 30" long. Be sure to purchase enough extra yarn.

Apple Picker's Basket-
Weave Poncho

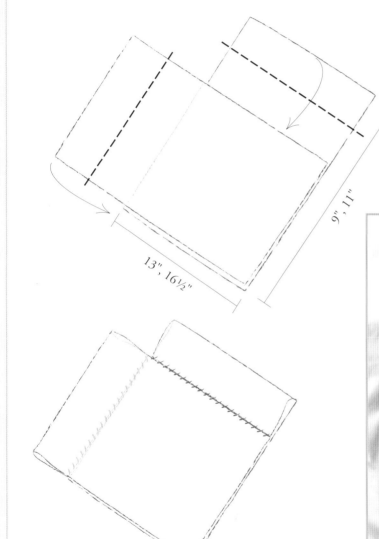

13", 16½"

9", 11"

Finishing

With wrong sides together, lay one strip over the second at right angles, matching edges at one corner. Fold end of top strip under to meet side edge of underlying strip and fold end of under strip forward to meet side edge of top strip as shown. Whip stitch the adjoining edges together, making sure each seam measures no more than 8 inches to allow a neck opening that is large enough to fit over a child's head.

Swing Coat

Are you going to a baby shower in a few days and wondering what you could knit in time? All in one piece, this cardigan is simple to knit and requires minimal finishing. Rather than increasing or decreasing, the shaping is accomplished by casting on and binding off. At less than 3 stitches to the inch and just two short seams to sew, beginners can complete this cardigan in a weekend or even a day. The plain fabric sets off a special single button you've been saving. Directions for the helmet begin on page 67.

Size

One size only, small (3-6 months)

Materials

Needles: 24"-long circular needle size 11 (8mm), or size needed to obtain correct gauge; crochet hook size I (5.5mm)

Yarn: Cascade Yarns, 2 skeins Bulky Leisure #8010 (Ecru)

Notions: 7/8"-diameter button

Gauge

11 sts and 20 rows = 4" in stockinette stitch

COAT

Back

Leaving an 18" tail, cast on 30 sts.

Rows 1 through 7: Knit.

Row 8 (WS): K1, purl to last st, k1.

Rows 9 through 22: Repeat rows 7 and 8.

Row 23: Cast on 15 sts at beg of row (begin right sleeve), knit across row (45 sts).

Row 24: Cast on 15 sts at beg of row (begin left sleeve), k3, purl to last 3 sts, k3 (60 sts).

Row 25: Knit.

Row 26: K3, purl to last 3 sts, k3.

Rows 27 through 38: Rep rows 25 and 26.

Right Front

Row 39: K22, k1 and leave the original stitch you knitted into on the left needle, turn work. Place sts from left needle onto a holder.

Rows 40 and 42 (WS): K2, p18, k3 (23 sts).

Rows 41 and 43: Knit.

Row 44: Cast on 2 sts at beg of row (neck shaping), k2, purl to last 3 sts, k3 (25 sts).

Row 45: Knit.

Row 46: Cast on 7 sts at beg of row, k9, purl to last 3 sts, k3, (32 sts).

Rows 47, 49 and 51: Knit.

Rows 48, 50 and 52: K3, purl to last 3 sts, k3.

Row 53: Bind off 15 sts at beg of row (end sleeve), knit to end (17 sts).

Row 54: K3, purl to last st, k1.

Row 55: Knit.

Rows 56 through 67: Repeat rows 54 and 55.

Rows 68 through 71: Knit.

Swing Coat with
Convertible Cloud
Helmet

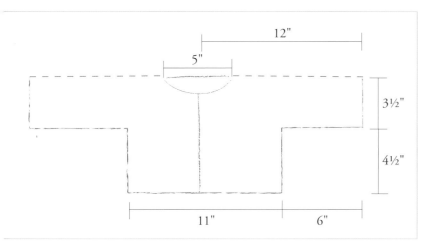

Row 46: K3, purl to last 9 sts, k9.

Rows 47, 49, 51, 53: Knit.

Rows 48, 50 and 52: K3, purl to last 3 sts, k3.

Row 54: Bind off 15 sts at beg of row (end sleeve), purl to last 3 sts, k3 (17 sts).

Row 55: Knit.

Row 56: K1, purl to last 3 sts, k3.

Rows 57-67: Repeat rows 55 and 56.

Rows 68-71: Knit.

Row 72 (WS): Bind off all sts.

Finishing

Fold work in half along "shoulders," right side out. Starting at hem edge, sew flat side seams. Fold garment inside out and starting at cuff edge, whip stitch sleeve seams.

Neck finishing: Pick up 36 sts evenly spaced around neck edge. Work two rows of garter stitch; bind off all sts. Or, if you prefer, work 2 rows of single crochet. Following the directions on page 51, crochet a chain long enough for the button to pass through when ends are held together. Cut yarn and draw end through the remaining loop to fasten off. Fold the chain in half to form a loop and, using the yarn tails, sew the loop ends to the left front edge at neck. Sew button to right front opposite button loop. Weave in yarn tails. Block carefully to measurements.

Row 72 (WS): Bind off all 17 stitches.

Left front

Place stitches from holder back onto needle. Join new yarn at right back neck, next to the stitches worked for the right front on the 39th row. Slip this st, k1, PSSO, cast off another 15 sts, (for back neck) knit to end (23 sts remain).

Continue on these 23 sts for left front, reversing neck and sleeve shaping to correspond to right front. (The right and left shaping will be mirror images.) Picking up with row 40, here are the full directions:

Rows 40, 42 and 44 (WS): K3, p18, k2.

Row 41: Knit.

Row 43: Cast on 2 sts at beg of row (neck shaping), knit to end (25 sts).

Row 45: Cast on 7 sts at beg of row, knit to end (32 sts).

Place stitches on a holder

Slip the stitches onto a stitch holder until you need to work them later. You can use a purchased holder, or simply thread a yarn length of a contrasting color in a yarn needle and pass it through the stitches. Remove the needle and tie the yarn ends together to keep the stitches securely on the yarn. When you need to work on these stitches again, slip them back onto the knitting needle, being careful to keep them in order and untwisted (remember, the right "leg" of the loop should be at the front of the needle; see "Looking at your work," page 33.

Convertible Cloud Helmet

The ear-flaps can tie over the top, "Sherlock Holmes-style," to convert this helmet (shown on the following page) to a hat on warmer days. I designed this cloud-like hat especially for those who want to learn how to knit in the round. To avoid purling and prevent inadvertently twisting when you join, you work the first 10 rows flat, knitting back and forth on straight needles every row to produce garter stitch. In circular knitting, stockinette fabric is formed by knitting every row; because you never turn your work, the right side is always facing you. Place a marker between the first and last stitches to mark the beginning of each round.

Sizes

3-6 months (6-12 months, 12-18 months) to fit up to 15" (17", 19") head

Materials

Needles: 16"-long circular needles size 9 (5.5mm) and size 10½ (6.5mm), 1 set of 5 double-pointed needles size 10½ (6.5mm), or sizes needed to obtain correct gauge

Yarn: Cascade Yarns,1 skein Bulky Leisure #8010 (Ecru)

Gauge

14 sts = 4" in stockinette stitch worked on larger needles

Knitting with Double-Pointed Needles

When you are decreasing and no longer have enough stitches to stretch around the circular needle, you'll need to transfer your work to a set of double-pointed needles (dpn). Divide your work evenly among four double-pointed needles and knit with the fifth. If the number of stitches is divisible by three instead of four, then it is more convenient to divide your work into thirds and knit with the fourth, especially when working shaping. To transfer the stitches to dp needles, slip the first third (or fourth) of the stitches onto one dpn, the next section onto a second dpn, etc., until each section is on its own separate dpn. (Retain one dpn for actual knitting.) Be sure the stitches are in the proper working order and are not twisted. Your work will now form a triangle or square depending on whether you are using three or four needles to hold the stitches. The empty additional dpn serves as your right needle and as you knit, you move the first needle stitches onto this additional needle. Use the newly emptied needle to knit off the stitches on the next needle. Continue to work around in this manner, and as you work, pull the working yarn tightly at the beginning of each needle to prevent a gap where loose tension creates ladders between the stitches.

Convertible Cloud Helmet

HELMET

Starting at lower edge of helmet, with smaller circular needle and leaving a 7" tail, cast on 40 (48, 56) sts. Do not join, but work back and forth, turning work at end of each row as if you were using straight needles.

Rows 1 through 10: Knit.

Rnd 11 (RS): To join at the end of the 10th row, keep the full end of needle in your right hand and bring the empty end of needle behind and around to your left hand. Place a marker for beg of rnds. Spread the stitches to the tip of the left needle and knit, connecting the work as you begin the 11th row.

Change to larger needles and work until hat measures 4" (4½", 5") above cast-on edge.

Next rnd: Transferring sts onto a double-pointed needle (dpn) *K3 (4, 5), k2tog, place marker, SSK, k3 (4, 5)*; repeat sequence onto across each of 3 more dpn.

Knit one rnd even. Repeat decrease rnd every other rnd, at the rate of 8 stitches per rnd by working k2tog before each marker and ssk after each marker. When you have 8 stitches left, cut yarn leaving a 12" tail. Use tapestry needle to draw yarn tail through all loops, going around twice. Pull gently to draw sts together. Fasten off. Sew flat seam to join garter st band.

Ear flaps

With smaller needle, starting 5 sts from back seam, pick up 12 (14, 16) sts from inside helmet where the garter stitch changes to reverse stockinette stitch, 1" from edge. Knit 8 rows. Then k2tog at beg of every row until there are 3 sts left. Work 7"-long I-cord (see page 41).

(see page 41).

To make **an adult version**, calculate your gauge and cast on enough stitches to equal one inch less than the wearer's head for a close fit. Measure the length by comparing it to an existing hat (about 8"-9" total). Begin decreasing about three inches from the top.

Bind-off row: K2tog, k1, PSSO. Make 2nd ear flap to correspond.

Finishing

Weave in yarn tails. Block lightly, if desired.

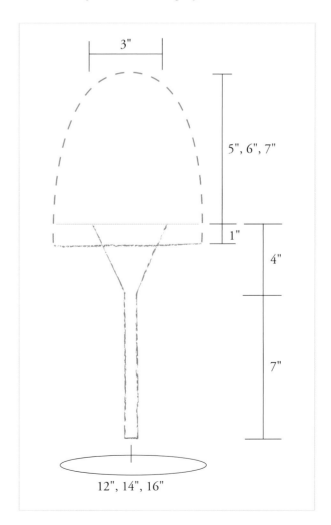

Flower Garden Blanket

ven beginners can knit a flower in an hour. The blanket itself will take a little longer, but it's still quite a fast project with a gauge of 3 stitches to the inch. Broad panels of stockinette stitch are enhanced by three cables and edged with garter stitch. Twist the cables every 10th row. Or if this is your first cable project, relax and twist them whenever it looks right and you will have a charmingly eccentric blanket. Follow the photo for flower placement or scatter them as you like. If a gift, consider giving the blanket with a single flower on it and then adding one every time you visit. You might like to "plant" several flower varieties by making smaller ones with finer yarn and needles and larger ones with bulkier yarn.

Size

About 27" wide by 33" long.

Materials

Needles: 24"-long circular needles size 9 (5.5mm) and size 10½ (6.5mm), or sizes needed to obtain correct gauge; cable needle

Yarn: Cascade Yarns, 3 skeins of Bulky Leisure #8010 (Ecru) for color A, 1 skein each of "220" #9442 (Baby Rose Heather) for color B and #7814 (Lime Heather) for color C

Gauge

12 sts = 4" on larger needle in stockinette st

Stitch pattern

Row 1 (RS): K2, *p2, k6, p2, k23; rep from*, end p2, k6, p2, k2.

Rows 2, 4, 6, 8, and 10: K2 then knit the k sts and purl the p sts as they face you, end k2.

Rows 3, 7, and 9: Repeat row 1.

Row 5: K2, *p2, slip 3 sts to cable needle and hold in front of work, k3, slip sts from cable needle back to left needle, k3 (3-by-3 front cable, FC, made), p2, k23; rep from*, end p2, 3-by-3 FC as before, p2, k2.

Repeat rows 1 through 10 for pattern.

Use scraps from your stash to make each flower a different color. (Test hand-dyed yarn, especially reds or other dark colors, for color-fastness before adding them to a light-colored blanket.) Children are delighted to see their first awkward attempts at knitting instantly transformed into a flower with a twist of the wrist and a few stitches to tack it down. This would be a lovely way to include an older child in making a blanket for a new sibling: Recruit her or him to help you make the flowers. While this version contains uniform flowers as a concession to those who prefer foreseeable results, you may prefer more organic flowers that are irregular and eccentric.

Flower Garden Blanket

AFGHAN

With Color A and smaller needle, leaving a 7" yarn tail, cast on 80 sts. Work back and forth on circular needle.

Work 6 rows garter st (knit every row). Change to larger needle and work 15 repeats of stitch pattern (150 rows), then work 8 more rows in stitch pattern. Change to smaller needles and work 6 rows garter stitch. Bind off with larger needle.

Flower (make 7)

With Color B and smaller needles, leaving an 18" yarn tail, cast on 7 sts.

Row 1: Knit.

Rows 2, 4, 6 and 8: Purl.

Row 3: *K1, yo, repeat from *, end k1 (13 sts).

Row 5: Repeat row 3 (25 sts).

Row 7: Knit.

Row 9: Bind off loosely with larger needle.

Leaf (make 14)

With Color C and smaller needles, leaving an 18" yarn tail, cast on 3 sts. Work 4 rows in stockinette st.

Row 5 (RS): K1, yo, k1, yo, k1.

Rows 6, 8, 10, 12, and 14: Purl.

Row 7: K2, yo, k1, yo, k2.

Row 9: K3, yo, k1, yo, k3.

Row 11: K4, yo, k1, yo, k4.

Row 13: Knit.

Row 15: Bind off.

Finishing

Starting at one side edge of flower piece, coil flower and tack together with a few stitches, sewing close to the base. Stitch leaves to the base of the flower. Attach flowers to quilt securely by working both flower tails through to the wrong side about ½" apart, tie in a square knot, work tails back through base of flower and repeat. Using the tail at the tip of the leaf, stitch the center of leaf to the blanket with running stitch. Weave in yarn tails.

Block lightly, if desired.

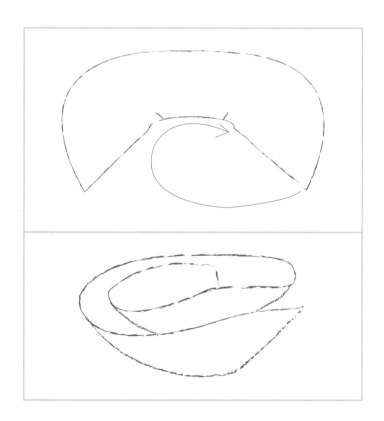

Seaside Stripes Tee-Shirt

This classic boat-neck pullover (shown on the following page) reminds me of French sailors and Picasso. The large gauge and uncomplicated construction make this an ideal beginner's project. The stripes are not just for style, they form an integral part of the pattern design. Counting the two-row stripes will help you to see more deeply the structure of knitted fabric.

After completing the identical front and back sections, begin picking up sleeve stitches at the indicated stripe. You will pick up 1 stitch in each blue stripe and 2 in each white stripe. When you come to the ribbed neckline, with right sides facing you, overlap the back over the front and pick up 6 stitches through both layers, and continue as before. The short sleeves are knitted quickly, so be sure to start decreasing right away. The side seams are good mattress stitch practice, especially if you match the stripes carefully.

The directions for a coordinating hat begin on page 76.

Sizes

3-6 months (6-12 months, 12-18 months)

Materials

Needles: 16"-long circular needles size 7 (4.5mm) and size 10½ (6.5mm), or size needed to obtain correct gauge; a straight needle size 3 for picking up sleeve sts

Yarn: Cascade Yarns, 1 skein each of Cotton Rich #2625 (Navy) for color A and #8176 (Natural) for color B

Gauge

16 sts = 4" in stockinette st on larger needles

TEE-SHIRT

Back

With color A and smaller circular needle, leaving 18" yarn tail, cast on 42 (46, 50) sts. Work 6 rows of 2-by 2-rib. Change to largest needle. Work in stockinette stitch, alternating 2 rows of each color until you have 50 (54, 62) rows or 25 (27, 31) stripes. Change back to smaller circular needles and color A. Work 10 rows of 2-by-2 ribbing. Bind off loosely with largest needle if needed.

Front

Work as for back.

Sleeves

With right side of both back and front facing up, place the neck edge of back over front neck edge, overlapping the rubbing. [Illus 36] At each side edge of sweater, pin the overlapped edges to hold them together. On one side edge, with the small straight needle and starting at the 11th (13th, 15th) stripe from neck edge, pick up 18 (21, 24) sts evenly spaced up to the ribbed section. Then working through both layers of overlapped ribbed section pick up 6 sts. Then

Seaside Stripes Tee-Shirt

pick up another 18 (21, 24) sts along edge down to 11th (13th, 15th) stripe below the neck for total of 42 (48, 54) sts. Starting with a purl row (on WS), change to largest needles and work in stockinette st, changing color every 2 rows and decreasing every knit row as follows: K2, ssk, knit to last 4 sts, k2tog, k2 until 28 (34, 40) sts remain. Change to smaller circular needles and work 6 rows in 2-by-2 ribbing.

Bind off loosely in ribbing (see page 32), using large needle if needed. Work second sleeve on opposite side in the same manner.

Finishing

Sew side seams using mattress stitch starting at the cuff and hem edges and working towards the center. Weave in yarn tails.

Block lightly, if desired.

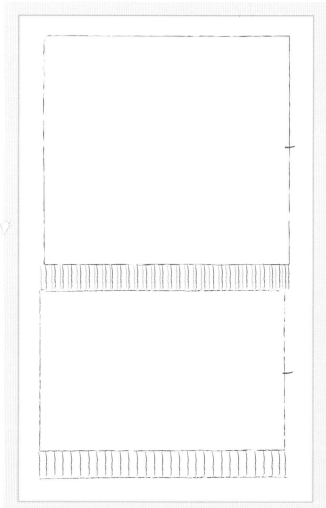

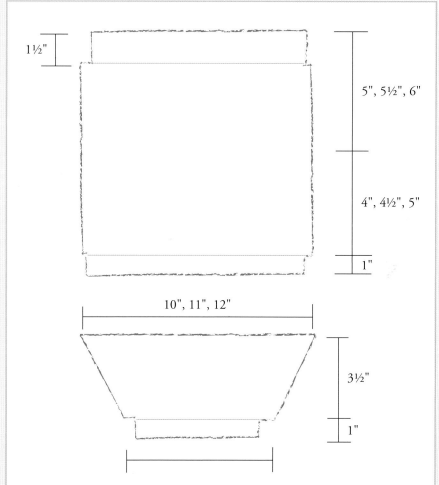

Seaside Stripes Sun Hat

Learning to handle double-pointed needles is easiest when you work from the bottom up, as for the Convertible Cloud Helmet (page 67). But you can also knit a hat from the top down, starting on double-pointed needles. The first few rounds may feel slow and awkward—until round 4, when you have 6 stitches per double pointed needle or 18 stitches total. To help you keep track of the shaping rounds, always increase on the second row of the two-row stripe pattern.

Sizes

Small (medium, large) to fit 14½" (16", 18") head

Materials

Needles: 16"-long circular needle and 1 set of 4 double-pointed needles size 7 (4.5mm), or sizes needed to obtain correct gauge; a straight needle size 9 (5.5mm) for binding off

Yarn: Cascade Yarns, 1 (1, 2) skein(s) each of Cotton Rich #8176 (Natural) for color A and #2625 (Navy) for color B

Gauge

20 sts = 4" on larger needles

HAT

Starting at top of hat, with Color A and leaving a 7" yarn tail, cast 6 sts onto 1 double-pointed needle. Divide sts evenly among 3 needles and knit with the fourth (see page 67).

Rnd 1: Join and knit 1 rnd.

Rnd 2: *Bar inc (k in front and back of st); rep from * (12 sts).

Rnd 3: Knit.

Rnd 4: *Place marker, inc, k1; rep from* (18 sts and 6 markers).

Rnd 5: Change to Color B and knit.

Rnd 6: *Slip marker, inc, k2; rep from *.

Rnd 7: Change colors and knit.

Rnd 8: *Slip marker, inc, knit to next marker; rep from * (6 sts increased on rnd).

Repeat last 2 rnds until there are 72 (78, 90) sts, changing to circular needle when you have enough sts

---

Alter this pattern for **adult sizes** by going up to a gauge of 3.5 stitches to the inch with the yarn doubled-stranded on a size 10½ (6.5mm) needle. Purchase enough extra yarn to complete. The sizing will fit correspondingly small, medium, and large adults. You can also adapt this pattern to flat knitting by casting on 2 extra stitches for a seam and purling the odd-numbered rows. The brim can easily be changed to a textured pattern, keeping continuity of pattern (see page 99). Because you can try it on as you go, it is an ideal project for improvising your own design.

Seaside Stripes Sun Hat

Knitting On The Go

Get in the habit of keeping your knitting with you and you'll be surprised at how fast your work progresses while you are doing other things such as watching TV, standing on line at the bank, riding the bus, or waiting for cookies to bake. Many of us don't have the luxury of sitting down to knit for an uninterrupted hour or two. However, if your schedule permits, you may find yourself knitting for hours on end. But be careful with your hands. Keep them relaxed and shake them out at least once an hour to prevent injury. A word about knitting etiquette: Though many knitters can actually pay better attention while knitting, unfortunately, it doesn't look that way to the uninitiated, especially at meetings. Unless you are sure your needles will be welcome, confine your knitting to breaks. Knitting at the movies, now rare, was commonplace in the 1930s and 40s. Be sensitive to your neighbors as some find the tiny movements of even the most discreet work distracting. I only knit at the movies if it is empty enough to sit alone, and then only with bamboo or plastic needles to avoid the clack and flash of metal.

to fit around the needle. Continuing to change colors every other row, knit even (without increasing) for 20 (24, 28) rnds to add 10 (12, 14) more stripes. Keep slipping markers each rnd so that the following brim increases will be aligned.

Brim

Next rnd: Continuing stripe pattern, *slip marker, inc, k11 (12, 14); rep from *.

Knit 1 rnd even.

Continuing stripes, increase every other rnd until there are 102 (108, 120) sts, ending with the final inc row.

Next rnd: Purl 1 rnd for a turning ridge. Do not change colors.

Decrease rnd: *Slip marker, k2tog, knit to next marker; rep from *.

Now continue with two-rnd stripe pattern as before, and work shaping as follows: Knit 1 rnd. Repeat decrease rnd. Repeat these last 2 rnds twice more, then knit 1 rnd even. Work a final decrease rnd and as you go,

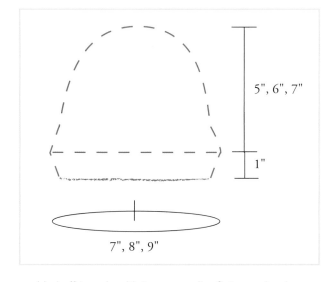

bind off loosely with larger needle. Cut yarn, leaving a 24" yarn tail.

Finishing

Fold brim at turning ridge and whip-stitch bound-off edge to inside of hat, matching stitch to stitch around starting rnd of brim. Weave in yarn tails.

Block lightly, if desired.

Buttercup Sundress

By attaching a fabric skirt to a knit top, you can make a dress in just a few hours. The bodice of this sundress (photo page 80) is knit in seed stitch—a nubby texture with good elasticity to accommodate fast growing babies and toddlers. Cross and uncross the straps in the back to adjust length.

The generous skirt hem also allows lengthening as needed. The shaping of the bodice is simplified by always eliminating multiples of 2 stitches at a time so as not to interrupt the pattern. Seed stitch is simplest when worked on an odd number of stitches so that you begin and end every row with k1.

Since the straps are narrow, you may wish to work them on short double-pointed needles as directed. Having the right tools for the job helps, but it is not necessary to transfer your work if you don't have double-pointed needles. This is one place where you can substitute a needle of a smaller size, though avoid using a larger needle.

Sizes

3-6 months (6-12 months, 12-18 months)

Note: the garment as shown is the 6-12 months size.

Materials

Needles: 16"-long circular needle size 7 (4.5mm), 2 double-pointed needles size 7 (4.5mm), or sizes needed to obtain correct gauge; a straight needle size 9 (5.5mm) for binding off; crochet hook size 7 (4.5mm)

Yarn: Cascade Yarns, 1 (2, 2) skeins of Cotton Rich #1317 (Buttercup)

Fabric: ½ yard 45" wide, for skirt

Notions: Three ⅝"-diameter buttons, sewing thread

Gauge

18 sts = 4" in stockinette st

Seed Stitch Pattern

Uneven number of sts.

Row 1: K1, *p1, k1; rep from *.

Repeat this row for pattern.

SUNDRESS

Knitted Bodice

Beginning at waist edge with smaller circular needles and leaving a 12" yarn tail, cast on 63 (73, 85) sts. Work in pattern until piece measure 3" (3½", 4"). Note: To make a more smoothly curved armhole without jogs, work each bind-off by slipping the first stitch instead of knitting it. At beg of next 2 rows, bind off 10 (12, 14) sts in pattern (see page 32; do not use larger needle). At beg of next 7 (9, 11) rows, bind off 2 sts [29 (31, 35) sts remain]. Next row (WS): Bind off 2 sts, work 9 sts in pattern (counting st left over from

Buttercup Sundress

binding off as first st), bind off in pattern (with larger needle) center 9 (11, 15) sts, work last 9 sts in pattern. Transfer these last 9 sts to a double-pointed needle (dpn), and set remaining sts still on circular needle aside.

Left strap: Working back and forth on 9 sts on dpn, continue in pattern and bind off 2 sts at beg of next 2 rows. Continue in pattern on 5 remaining sts for 4½" (5", 5½").

Buttonhole: K1, p1, yo, p2tog, k1. Work 4 more rows in pattern. Bind off.

Right strap: Transfer 9 sts from circular needle to dpn and work same as for left strap.

Finishing

With sewing thread, sew a button to each side of back ½" below top edge and 1" (1½", 2") from back edge. Sew the third button to the right back edge, next to the first. Crochet a chain for button loop according to directions on page 51, and attach to the left corner. Weave in yarn tails.

Block lightly, if desired.

Skirt

Cut a rectangle of fabric approximately twice as wide as the bodice plus 1" on each side, or 30" (38", 44") by 12½" (14", 16") deep. Fold over 1" at each end and hem. Then, gather the waist by working two rows of hand or machine basted stitches ¼" apart, about ½" from one long edge of fabric. Adjust gathering to fit bodice, pinning skirt in place, and then hand or machine stitch to secure. Hem bottom edge, using 4" hem allowance or amount desired.

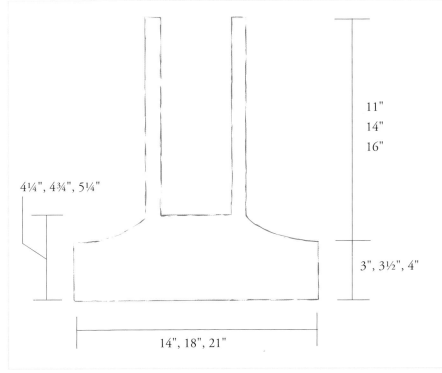

11"
14"
16"

4¼", 4¾", 5¼"

3", 3½", 4"

14", 18", 21"

Victorian Eyelet Sundress

Here is another fast dress top, this time worked from side seam to side seam in garter stitch so that the ridges run vertically. This technique, worked on a tight gauge, yields fabric with a good deal of stretch. The eyelet edging is worked separately and sewn on. This edging is much simpler than most found in stitch pattern books; it has been designed so you will learn the pattern quickly. If you want to knit an eyelet hem, purchase another skein and work sufficient repeats to fit around the hem edge.

Sizes
3-6 months (6-12 months, 12-18 months)

Materials
Needles: 16"-long circular needle size 7 (4.5mm), or size needed to obtain correct gauge; 1 pair straight needles size 9 (5.5mm) for eyelet border; crochet hook size 7 (4.5 mm)

Yarn: Cascade Yarns, 1 (2, 2) skeins of Cotton Rich #8176 (Natural)

Fabric: ½ yard 45" wise, for skirt

Notions: Three ⅝"-diameter buttons, sewing thread

Gauge
18 sts and 40 rows = 4" on smaller needle in garter stitch

Eyelet Edging Stitch Pattern
Note: Edging is worked sideways.

Row 1 (RS): K1, yo, k2.
Rows 2, 4, 6 and 8: Knit.
Row 3: K1, yo, k1, yo, k2.
Row 5: K1, yo, k3, yo, k2.
Row 7: Bind off 5 sts at beg of row, knit to end.
Repeat rows 1 through 8 for pattern.

EYELET DRESS
Bodice

Beginning at center back edge with circular needle and leaving a 12" yarn tail, cast on 15 (20, 25) sts. Work in garter stitch until piece measures 3" (4", 5"), or 30 (40, 50) rows. Inc 1 st at one edge (top edge) every other row 5 (7, 9) times. At same (top) edge, cast on 30 (40, 50) sts for left shoulder strap [50 (67, 84) sts remain]. Knit 3 rows even. Next row (buttonhole row): K to last 6 sts, *yo, k2tog, k 1; rep from * once more (2 buttonholes made at end of strap). Knit 2 rows even. Bind off 25 (30, 35) sts at beg of next row, knit to end of row. Knit 1 row. Dec at top edge every other row 5 (7, 9) times, [20 (30, 40) sts remain]. Work even for 10 rows for center front of bodice. Inc 1 st at top edge every other row 5 (7, 9) times. Then at top edge, cast on 25 (30, 35) sts for second shoulder strap. Work 3 rows even. Work buttonhole row as for first strap. Work 2 rows even. Bind off 30 (40, 50) sts at beg of next row, knit to end

Victorian Eyelet Sundress

of row. Knit 1 more row. Dec 1 st at top edge every other row 5 (7, 9) times, [15 (20, 25) sts remain]. Knit 30 (40, 50) rows more. Bind off all sts loosely.

Neck edging

With larger needles, leaving a 12" yarn tail, cast on 3 sts. Work 14 (16, 18) repeats of stitch pattern or until long enough to edge neckline and straps. Bind off remaining sts.

Finishing

With sewing thread, sew a button to each side of back ½" below top edge and 1" (1½", 2") from back edge. Sew the third button to the right back edge, next to the first. Crochet a chain for button loop according to directions on page 51, and attach to the left corner. Weave in yarn tails.

Block lightly, if desired.

Skirt

Cut a rectangle of fabric approximately twice as wide as the bodice plus 1" on each side, or 30" (38", 44") by 12½" (14", 16") deep. Fold over 1" at each end and hem. Then, gather the waist by working two rows of hand or machine basted stitches ¼" apart, about ½" from one long edge of fabric. Adjust gathering to fit bodice, pinning skirt in place and then hand or machine stitch to secure. Hem bottom edge, using 4" hem allowance or amount desired.

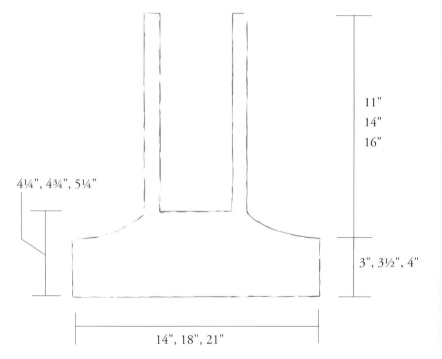

Origami Kimono and Bloomers

Here's another side-to-side garment, worked in one piece from cuff to cuff. Garter stitch worked sideways creates an easy-to-knit vertical ridge that curves gracefully over the shoulders. With only increasing, decreasing, casting on and off, the construction is minimal. Maximum wearing time is factored into the design, which works both oversized at first and cropped and fitted later.

At six years of age I learned to fold origami cranes in addition to knitting. Now I fold my knitting into origami; you may feel you are doing the same when you are knitting this kimono. So unlikely and octopus-like is the work in progress that you may wonder how it will become a sweater. Because garter stitch looks the same on both sides, tie a bow around a safety pin and attach it to the piece you designate as the right side, then at each stage, compare the outline of your garment with the bird's eye view at right. The double ties give you the option to use either the left or the right front on top when you overlap the fronts.

If you wish, you can substitute a few rows of single crochet instead of picking up stitches around the neck (see page 51).

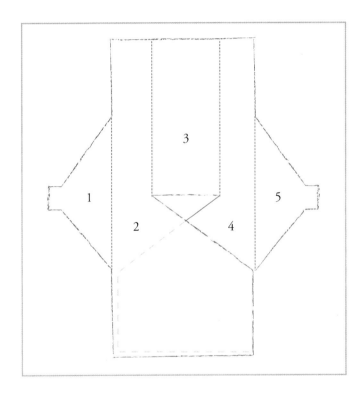

Sizes

3-6 months (6-12 months, 12-18 months)
Note: the garment shown is the 6-12 month size.

Kimono Materials

Needles: 24"-long circular needle size 7 (4.5mm), or size

Origami Kimono
and Bloomers

needed to obtain correct gauge; a straight needle size 9 (5.5mm) for binding off (optional); crochet hook size 7 (4.5mm)

Yarn: Cascade Yarns, 3 (4, 5) skeins of Pima Tencel #7013 (Teal)

Notions: 2 stitch holders (or use yarn needle and contrasting yarn)

Gauge

20 sts and 36 rows = 4" in garter st

KIMONO

Right sleeve

Starting at cuff of right sleeve (shown as section 1 on bird's eye view) with smaller needles and leaving a 24" yarn tail, cast on 30 sts for all sizes. Knit 10 (14, 18) rows. At beg of next and every following row, k in front and back of first st (bar inc) until there are 70 (76, 82) sts.

Body

Cast on and then knit 20 (22, 24) sts at beg of next 2 rows for front and back side (underarm) edges [110 (120, 130) sts on needle; section 2 begun]. Knit 20 (30, 40) rows even. Next row: K55 (60, 65) sts for right front and turn. Place remaining back sts on a holder. Work right front only, starting at WS of neck edge and decreasing 1 st at beg of this and every other row until 25 (30, 35) sts remain. Bind off all remaining sts loosely, using larger needle if needed.

Left front

Cast on 25 (30, 35) sts and knit 1 row. Inc (bar method) 1 st at beg of this and every WS row at neck edge until you have 55 (60, 65) sts. Place these sts on a second holder to be continued as section 4.

Back

Place back sts from holder onto needle, being careful not to twist stitches. Knit 30 rows for section 3. Join left front to back at beg of next row [110 (120, 130) sts]. Knit 20 (30, 40) rows even for section 4. Bind off 20 (22, 24) sts at beg of next 2 rows [70 (76, 82) sts remain for left sleeve (section 5)].

Left sleeve

K2tog at beg of next and every following row until 30 sts remain. Knit 10 (14, 18) rows for cuff. Bind off loosely.

Crocheted ties

Leaving 12" yarn tail, use crochet hook to chain 50 (see page 51). Fasten off last loop. Repeat for second tie. Weave yarn tail through chain to the mid-point and attach a tie to side edge of each front, just below sleeve.

Finishing

Fold garment along "shoulders" and sew flat side seams from sleeve cuff to underarm, and from hem to underarm using yarn tails, and leaving a small hole in the seam where you attached the ties, so that the ties can be used either on the inside or the outside of the garment.

With smaller needles and right side of work facing you, starting at right front neck edge, pick up 1 stitch in each trough along the shaped garter stitch neck edge, continue around back neck still working 1 stitch per trough, and then along the left front neck edge. Knit 4 rows and bind off loosely. Block garment carefully

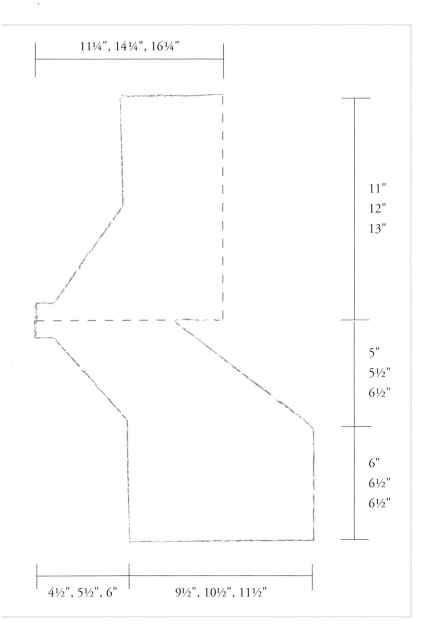

11¼", 14¼", 16¼"

11"
12"
13"

5"
5½"
6½"

6"
6½"
6½"

4½", 5½", 6"   9½", 10½", 11½"

using schematic measurements (above). To fasten, overlap fronts and poke one end of each tie through neck edging.

BLOOMERS

Knit bloomers in a matching or contrasting color to coordinate with the Origami Kimono. In addition to functioning as a fashionable cover-up over diapers, this pattern can also be used to make woolen soakers. Though hard to conceive, disposable diapers are a relatively new invention. Prior to that, woolen "soakers" helped wick away moisture, keeping cloth diapers in place. While older generations of moms still recoil at the memory of endless laundering, some moms are enthusiastic about the environmental and hygienic benefits of the old-fashioned approach.

Each short leg is worked flat and started separately, then soon joined to be worked in stockinette stitch in the round on a 16" circular needle, a pleasant and relaxing knit. For pants to fit well, the front must be lower than the back. After working 1½" of ribbing, you will cease knitting in the round so that you can gradually decrease stitches from each side of the waist to make the back part of the waistband higher than the front part.

Sizes

3-6 months (6-12 months, 12-18 months)
Note: the garment shown is the 6-12 months size.

Bloomers Materials

Needles: 16"- or 24"-long circular needles size 5 (3.75mm) and size 7 (4.5mm), or size needed to maintain correct gauge

Yarn: Cascade Yarns, 2 (3, 3) skeins of Pima Tencel #7013 (Teal)

Notions: 1 yard of 5/8"-wide elastic, sewing thread

Gauge

20 sts = 4" in stockinette st on larger needle

BLOOMERS

Leg band: With smaller circular needle and leaving a 10" yarn tail, cast on 41 (45, 49) sts. Do not join, but work back and forth on circular needle. Knit 6 rows. Change to larger needle and k13 (15, 17) sts, bar inc (k in front and back of st) in each of next 15 sts, k13 (15, 17) [56 (60, 64) sts total]. Knitting first and last st of every row for garter st selvage, work 4 (6, 8) rows in stockinette st. Cut yarn and set first piece aside; work a second leg band.

Place both leg bands on needle with RS facing you, to join as one piece [112 (120, 128) sts total].

Next row: Work in stockinette st in the round and place markers as follows: k28 (30, 32), place marker for side, k56 (60, 64), place marker for other side, k28 (30, 32). There are 56 (60, 64) sts each for front and back sections between markers. Continue in stockinette st until piece measures 6½" (7½", 8½") from cast-on edge.

Change to smaller needle and work 1½" in 2-by-2 ribbing for waistband. Begin back waistband shaping as follows.

Next row: Continuing in ribbing, work through 18th (20th, 22nd) st after first marker, bind off 20 center front sts, complete row. Now work back and forth in rows as flat

knitting, and bind off 4 sts at beginning over every row 12 times [44 (52, 60) sts remain]. Loosely bind off remaining sts, leaving a 36" yarn tail.

Finishing

Cut elastic to 16½" (18½", 20½"), overlap ends by ½" and sew them together securely with sewing thread. Fold top half of ribbed waistband to inside, enclosing elastic ring. Loosely whip-stitch bound-off edge to beginning row of ribbing. Sew each leg inseam using flat seam. Weave in yarn tails.

Block lightly, if desired.

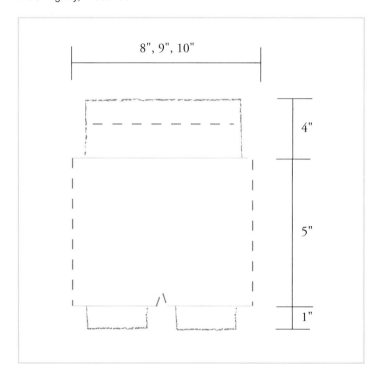

Hibiscus Hooded Zip Jacket and Accessories

Knitting two or more strands of yarn together is easy—just hold them together and knit as if they were one strand. This produces a tweedy effect in which the colors randomly dominate each other. By blending yarns, you can achieve a unique palette of brand new colors, which adds an interesting touch to a plain garment like—this oversize jacket. A dark and a light color yarn combined make a high-contrast pattern. Two yarns of similar color and hue will make a subtle yet rich fabric. Experiment with various pairings until you find one that pleases you.

Sizes

3-6 months (6-12 months, 12-18 months)
Note: the garment shown is the 6-12 months size.

SUPER SIMPLE SOCKS

Turning a conventional sock heel has its charm but there is an easier way: knit a tube straight down and set aside the heel stitches by knitting them onto scrap yarn (use a contrasting color). After decreasing for the toe, remove the scrap yarn and pick up the original number of stitches as shown in the drawing. Work a second "toe" for the heel shaping.

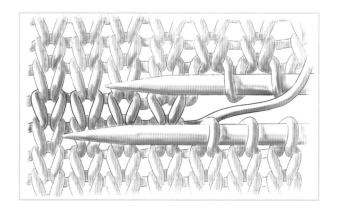

Decreasing at the rate of four stitches per round is easy to keep track of if you divide your work onto four double-pointed needles and knit with a fifth. Of course you can adapt this method for adult socks by changing the gauge or number of stitches cast on and working for sufficient length. Be sure to use reinforcing nylon for the heels and toes if you are knitting in pure wool for extended wear.

Sizes

up to 9 months (18 months)
Note: the garment shown is the larger size.
Materials
Needles: 1 set each of 5 double-pointed needles size 5

Hibiscus Hooded
Zip Jacket and
Accessories with
color variation

(3.75mm) and size 7 (4.5mm), or size needed to obtain correct gauge

Yarn: Cascade Yarns, 1 skein each of 128 Tweed #7608 (Pink) for color A and #7605 (Orange/Red) for color B

Gauge

17 sts = 4" in stockinette st with single strand of yarn on larger needles

SOCKS

Starting at top ribbing with smaller needles and a single strand of color A and leaving a 7" yarn tail, cast on 24 (28) sts. Divide sts evenly onto 3 needles.

Join sts as you begin work, placing a marker to indicate beginning of round.

Work 17 (22) rnds in 2-by-2 ribbing.

Change to larger needles and color B and knit 11 (14) rnds even in stockinette stitch.

Next rnd: K12 (14) sts with contrasting scrap yarn and slip them back onto your left needle. Knit the 12 (14) scrap yarn stitches with your original yarn, knit remaining sts of rnd.

Knit 11 (14) rnds even.

Toe shaping: Redistribute stitches evenly onto 4 dpn and knit with the fifth: sl marker at beginning of round, ssk, k8 (10), k2tog, place marker, ssk, k8 (10), k2tog [20 (24) sts remain]. Knit 1 rnd even. Decrease before and after each marker every other rnd as set until 16 sts remain, then decrease every round until 4 sts remain. Cut yarn and draw through loops.

Heel shaping: Remove scrap yarn, placing stitches on 4 dpn. Make sure you pick up 12 (14) sts both above and below scrap yarn [24 (28) sts total]. On first rnd, pick up 1 st in the side gap, k12 (14), pick up 2 sts at second side gap, placing marker between those 2 sts, k12 (14), pick up 1 st at first side gap and place marker [28 (32) sts total].

Next rnd: *Slip marker, k2tog, knit to 2 sts before next

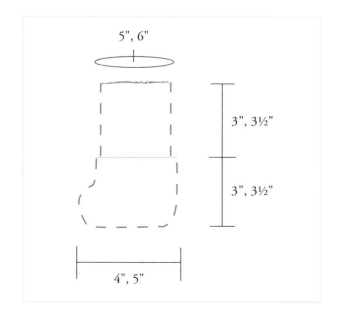

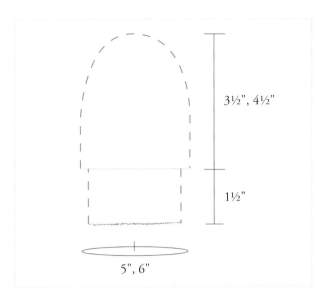

marker, ssk* repeat once more. Knit 1 rnd. Continue as for toe shaping.

Make another sock to match.

Finishing

Weave in yarn tails. Block lightly, if desired.

Jacket and Mittens Materials

Needles: 16"- or 24"-long circular needles size 10½ (6.5mm), and 11 (8mm), 1 set each of double-pointed needles size 5 (3.75mm) and size 7 (4.5 mm), or sizes needed to obtain correct gauge; crochet hook size I (5.5mm)

Yarn: Cascade Yarns, 3 (4, 4) skeins each of 128 Tweed #7608 (Pink) for color A and #7605 (Orange/Red) for color B

Notions: Separating jacket zipper 8" (9", 10") long; five stitch holders

Gauge

For jacket

12 sts = 4" in stockinette st with double stand of yarn on larger needle

For mittens

17 sts = 4" in stockinette with single strand of yarn on larger needle

THUMBLESS MITTENS

Starting at cuff with smaller double-pointed needles (dpn) and a single strand of color A and leaving a 7" yarn tail, cast on 24 (28) sts. Divide sts evenly onto 3 dpm. Join sts as you begin work, placing a marker to indicate beginning of round.

Work 10 rounds in 2-by-2 ribbing. Change to larger dpn and color B and work 17 (22) rounds in stockinette st.

Tip shaping: Redistribute stitches evenly onto 4 dpn and knit with the fifth: sl marker at beginning of the round, ssk, k8 (10), k2tog, place marker, ssk, k8 (10), k2tog [20 (24) sts remain]. Knit 1 rnd even. Decrease before and after each marker every other rnd as set until 16 sts remain, then decrease every round until you have 4 sts remaining. Cut yarn and draw through loops.

Finishing

For each mitten, use crochet hook and cast-on tail to

crochet a chain of 8 sts (see page 51) and attach end to cuff to form button loop. Weave in yarn tails.

JACKET

My students often ask about putting in zippers, and many decide not to after I explain my method, deciding buttonholes aren't so hard after all. I designed this jacket to encourage you to learn how to put in a zipper under ideal circumstances. You can install your first zipper perfectly if you carefully follow the directions in the Course, under Finishing, page 50.

Back

Start at lower edge with smaller circular needles and one strand each of A and B held together. Leaving an 18" yarn tail, cast on 32 (36, 40) sts. Do not join sts but work back and forth as follows.

Row 1 (RS): K1, *k2, p2; rep from *, end k2, k1.

Row 2: K1, *p2, k2; rep from *, end p2, k1.

Repeat rows 1 and 2 four more times. Change to larger needles.

Next row (RS): K1, bar inc (k in front and back of next st) for small size only (no shaping for medium size, k2tog for large size), knit to end [33 (36, 39) sts total]. Starting with a purl row, work in stockinette st (always knitting the first and last st of every row for garter stitch selvage) until back measures 10" (11", 12") from cast-on edge. Mark side edges for armholes at 4½" (5", 5½") from beg. Place first 9 (9, 11) sts on a holder for one shoulder, center 15 (18, 17) sts for back of neck on another holder, and last 9 (9, 11) sts for shoulder on a third holder.

Right front

With smaller needles and one strand each of A and B held together, leaving an 18" yarn tail, cast on 16 (16, 20) sts.

Row 1 (RS): K1, *k2, p2; rep from *, end k3.

Row 2: K1, *p2, k2; rep from *, end p2, k1.

Repeat rows 1 and 2 four more times.

Change to larger circular needles. For 6-12 months size only, inc 1 st next row as follows: k1, bar inc, knit to end [16 (17, 20) sts total]. Continue working in stockinette st (always knitting the first and last stitch of every row) until work measures 8½" (9½", 10½") from cast-on edge. Mark side edges for armhole at 4½" (5", 5½") from beginning.

Neck shaping: Bind off 4 sts at beginning of next RS row. Bind off 3 (4, 5) sts at beginning of following RS row. Work even on 9 (9, 11) sts until piece measures same as back. Place remaining st on holder.

Left front

Work same as for right front until work measures 8½" (9½", 10½") from cast-on edge. Mark side edge for armholes.

Neck shaping: Bind off 4 sts at beginning of next WS row. Bind off 3 (4, 5) sts at beginning of following WS row. Work even on 9 (9, 11) sts until piece measures same as back. Place remaining sts on holder.

Shoulder Seams: Join fronts to back using three-needle bind-off; keep remaining 15 (18, 17) center back sts on holder for hood.

Sleeves

Starting at armhole markers with RS of work facing

you and using smaller needles, pick up 28 (30, 32) sts evenly spaced between armhole markers (about every 2 rows). Change to larger needles. Next row: k1, p bar inc (purl in front and back of stitch), p to last 2 sts, p bar inc, end k1 [30 (32, 36) sts total]. Work 2 (4, 0) more rows in stockinette st (knitting the first and last stitch of every row for garter stitch border). Decrease row (RS): K2, ssk, knit to last 4 sts, k2tog, k2. Repeat decrease row every 4th row until 22 sts remain, ending with a WS row.

Ribbing: Change to smaller needles. Next row (RS): K1, *k2, p2; rep from *, end k3.

Following row (WS): K1, p1, k2, *p2, k2; rep from *, end k1. Repeat these last two rows twice more. Bind off loosely, leaving an 18" yarn tail.

Hood

Cast on and then knit 15 (15, 17) sts, knit jacket back neck sts from holder. Cast on and then knit 15 (15, 17) sts, knit across to end [45 (48, 51) sts total]. Work 5" (5½", 6") in stockinette (always knitting the first and last 3 stitches of every row to form 3-stitch garter stitch border). End with a WS row. Bind off 15 (15, 17) sts at beginning of next 2 rows [15 (18, 17) sts remain]. Continue in stockinette st for 20 (24, 28) rows, working a 1-stitch garter stitch border on each edge. Work 5 rows in garter stitch. Bind off loosely.

Finishing

Sew cast-on edges of hood to front neck edges and continue sewing to join the open edges on each side of hood. Sew flat side and sleeve seams. Weave in yarn tails. Install zipper using the instructions on page 50.

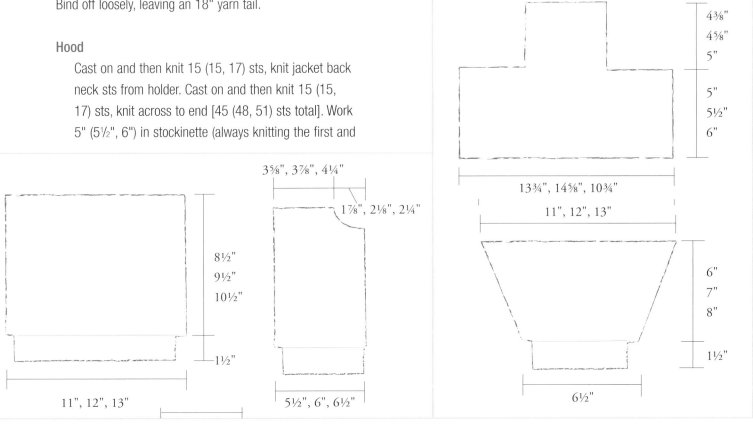

A little history

No one knows exactly when and where knitting was invented. Humans have likely been tying knots and interconnecting loops to make garments and home accessories for thousands of years. Our rich history of needle arts is evidenced by literally countless ways to manipulate fiber: macramé, bobbin lace, hairpin lace, basketry, weaving, tatting, netting, braiding, felting, embroidery, needlepoint, cross-stitch, and of course, knitting and crochet. *Naalbinding,* currently making a quiet comeback, is formed by sewing rows of loops together making a fabric that looks similar to crochet. The earliest known examples of *naalbinding* are 6th century BC Egyptian socks, followed by northern European examples dating back to the 10th century AD. While knitting, or a near cousin, might have developed more than 2,000 years ago, the earliest known examples of modern knitting are two finely knit pillows, richly patterned with fleur-de-lis, bird, clover, and castle motifs, which date from 13th century Spain. The work is so accomplished that the knitter must have learned from the experience of many generations before. Many consider the height of knitting was reached during the Italian Renaissance by master knitters—men trained for 6 years in the guilds while nuns perfected the art of lace in convents.

From that time on we find knitting flourishing throughout the globe from Scandinavia, the British Isles, Eastern Europe, Asia, South America, and North America. Each community of knitters developed its own techniques and traditions while constantly incorporating new influences and inspirations. By the mid-16th century, after receiving a pair of silk stockings as a gift, Queen Elizabeth of England started the first modern knitting craze by refusing to wear anything else (traditional leg coverings were cut on the bias from woolen cloth). The new knitted stockings were so popular that little else was knitted until the late 18th century. Stocking knitting was a part of daily life for men, women, and children of both sexes. Women often completed a sock every day, the surplus beyond family needs providing much-needed income. The long marches of the American Revolutionary and Civil Wars created an endless need for socks, which mothers, wives, daughters, and sisters knit not only to warm feet but also as tangible reminders of loved ones at home.

During WWI and WWII, the Red Cross and yarn companies sponsored knitting events and teaching centers to train new generations of knitters and provide our soldiers with "luxury" items such as hats, scarves, sweaters, and socks. WWII left many knitters "knitted out" which may have attributed to the "decline" of knitting until it was once again "rediscovered" in the 1960s and 70s.

When asked how long the current trend in knitting will last, the only gap I see in knitting's consistent popularity is the mid-20th century one in which knitting as a pastime was the exception, not the rule. People of all ages and diverse backgrounds are again discovering the satisfaction of making something with their own hands. With every stitch you make, you are carrying on the art of an ageless tradition. I predict all the needle arts will continue to flourish throughtout the 21st century and beyond.

Middlebury V-Neck Pullover

The indescribable red of Vermont foliage inspired this classic pullover, handsome enough for any college-bound infant. The stitch pattern is easy to work: knit across the right side, work ribbing on the wrong side. The garter stitch border facilitates fast seaming using the flat method. The front neck is self-finishing; the back neck band is worked at a 90-degree angle to the center back neck stitches.

Sizes

6-12 months (12-18 months)

Materials

Needles: 24"-long circular needles size 9 (5.5mm) and size 10½ (6.5mm), or sizes needed to obtain correct gauge; 3 straight or double-pointed needles size 10½ (6.5mm) for 3-needle bind off

Yarn: Cascade Yarns, 2 (3) skeins of Bulky Leisure #9404 (Ruby)

Notions: 5 stitch holders (or use yarn needle and scrap yarn)

Gauge

12 sts = 4" in stockinette st on larger needle

Stitch Pattern

Multiple of 5 (6) sts, plus 2

Row 1 (RS): Knit.

Row 2: *K2, p 3 (4); repeat from * across, end k2.
Repeat these 2 rows for pattern.

PULLOVER

Back

Starting with smaller circular needle and leaving an 18" yarn tail, cast on 32 (38) sts. Working back and forth on circular needle, work 6 rows in pattern. Change to larger circular needle and work 42 (50) more rows in pattern. Place first 10 (12 sts) sts on a holder for shoulder, center 12 (14) sts on a separate holder for back neck, and last 10 (12) sts on a third holder for other shoulder.

Front

Work as for back, completing 24 (28) rows, or until work measures about 5½" (6½") from beg.

Left neck shaping: Divide work on next row (RS) as follows: K16 (19), bar inc (k in front and back of st) [18 (21) sts now on right needle]; turn work. Place remaining 15 (18) sts on a holder for right front while you complete left front.

Row 26 (30): K3, p 3 (4), continue in pattern as established (see box on next page).

97

Middlebury V-Neck Pullover

Working in pattern as established:

To keep the continuity of the pattern as you increase or decrease stitches at the edge of your work, you need to remember that the pattern repeats at the shaped edge are changed as you add or subtract the stitches. For instance, if you decreased with "k2tog," the first stitch is gone, the second stitch is the remaining k stitch and the next stitch to be worked is the third stitch of the pattern repeat, so work it as the third pattern stitch, just as if there had been no decrease. At the beginning of shaped rows, you are working the end stitches of the ever-shrinking pattern repeat; at the end of shaped rows you are working the beginning stitches of the shrinking pattern repeat.

When you increase stitches (as on sleeves), you are *adding* new pattern repeats at the edges. The first stitch added (at beg of row) is the last stitch of the new pattern repeat, which will "grow" outward. The last stitch added (at end of row) is the first stitch of a new repeat.

Place markers for each pattern repeat until you become familiar with working increases and decreases in pattern. Following a chart (or making your own chart) of the pattern repeat makes it easier to visualize the pattern at the shaped edges. Knitting charts use a dash for a purl stitch, a vertical line for a knit stitch.

Row 27 (31): Knit to last 5 sts, k2tog, k3.
Work 3 rows even. Continue in this manner, maintaining 3-stitch garter stitch border at neck edge, and working dec on last 2 sts before border on next and then every 4th row until 13 (15) sts remain, ending on a WS row. Bind off 3 border sts and place remaining 10 (12) sts on a holder for shoulder.

Right front neck shaping, row 25 (29): Cast on 3 sts for neck edge and knit across row [18 (21) sts].

Row 26 (30): Work in pattern as established, end k3.

Row 27 (31): K3, ssk, knit to end.
Maintaining 3-st garter stitch border at neck edge, continue to dec 1 st at neck every 4th row to correspond to left front. When right side is completed, do not bind off the 3 border sts, but place them on a separate holder (bobby pin or paper clip). Transfer 10 (12) left shoulder sts for front and back from holders to separate straight needles, and with RS together, bind off, using three-needle bind-off (see page 48). In same manner, bind off right shoulder sts.

Sleeves

With scrap yarn or safety pins, mark side edges on front and back at 4" (5") from cast-on edge. With larger circular needle and RS of work facing you, pick up 32 (38) sts evenly spaced along armhole edge between markers, roughly 1 st in each garter stitch "trough." Do not join sts but work back and forth as follows.

Row 1 (WS): K7 (8), p3 (4), *k2, p3 (4); repeat from *, end k7 (8).

Row 2: Knit.

For large size only: Work 8 rows more in pattern as established.

For both sizes: Next row: K2tog, knit to last 2 sts, k2tog. Maintaining pattern as established, repeat decrease row every 4th row until 20 (24) sts remain. Change to smaller circular needle and work 6 more rows in pattern. Bind off with larger needles. Cut yarn leaving 18" tail.

Finishing

Back neck edge: Slip back neck sts and then the 3 right front border sts from holders on to smaller needle with RS facing you (border sts should be at tip of needle when held in left hand, ready to knit). Join yarn and work as follows: K2, knit together 1 st from 3-st border and 1 st from back, turn. Next row: Knit, turn. Repeat these 2 rows until 3 sts remain. Bind off.

Sew to bound-off edge of left front neck edge. Sew flat seams for sleeves and sides and weave in yarn tails. Block lightly, if desired.

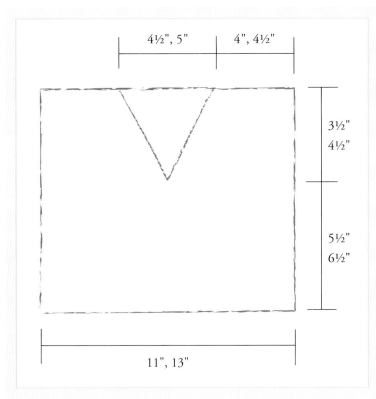

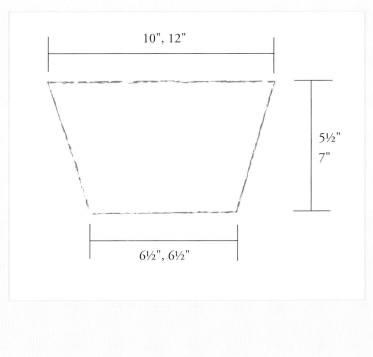

Black and White
Mobile and Rattle

Babies respond well to the high contrast of black and white stripes. This mobile, shown on page 102, is designed to introduce you to knitting three-dimensional objects: a sphere, a cube, a pyramid, and a rod. Be sure to hang the mobile out of baby's reach. The rattle combines two spheres and a rod.

Your imagination will suggest ways to use these basic shapes to create any kind of object or sculpture you want. To see what I mean, try a variation of the rod and sphere used to make a simple and charming toy bunny (page 108). Or make big blocks and pillows by increasing the stitch and row counts. Trust your instincts and keep asking "What happens if I try this?"

Materials

Needles: 1 pair of straight needles size 7 (4.5mm), or size needed to obtain correct gauge

Yarn: Cascade Yarns, 1 skein each of Cotton Rich #8990 (Dark Noon) for color A and #8176 (Natural) for color B

Notions: Two small jingle bells for rattle; 10 feet of fishing line; 36" length of $3/8$"-diameter wooden dowel; black spray paint

Gauge

18 sts = 4" in garter stitch

ROD

With Color A, leaving a 12" yarn tail, cast on 9 sts. Knit 2 rows. Change to Color A and knit 2 rows. Work a total of 30 rows, changing color every other row as established.

Bind off.

CUBE

First side: Work as for first 18 rows of rod. Bind off.

Make 5 more sides.

SPHERE

With Color A, leaving a 12" yarn tail, cast on 5 sts. Knit 2 rows.

Row 3: With Color B, *bar inc (k in front and back of st); repeat from * once more, end k1 (9 sts on needle).

Row 4 and all even-numbered rows: Knit.

Row 5: With Color A, repeat row 3 (17 sts).

Row 7: With Color B, *bar inc, k1; rep from *, end k2 (25 sts).

Rows 9 through 16: Work even, changing color every other row as established.

Row 17: With Color A, *k2tog, k1; repeat from *, end k2 (17 sts).

Black and White Mobile

Make any of these shapes from **any scrap of yarn** and stuff with catnip for homemade cat toys.

Row 19: With Color B, *k2tog repeat from *, end k1, (9 sts).

Row 21: With Color A, rep row 19 (5 sts). Bind off.

PYRAMID

With Color A, leaving a 12" yarn tail, cast on 11 sts. Knit 21 rows, changing colors every other row. Next row (WS): Cast on 33 sts at beginning of row, k to end (44 sts). With Color B, begin decreasing at the rate of 8 sts every other RS row as follows: *ssk, k7, k2tog, place marker, repeat from * three more times (36 sts). Knit 1 row. Change to Color A and knit 2 rows. Continue in this manner, changing color every other row and dec 1 st each side of each marker on the next and then every 4th row. When 12 sts remain, change to color A and k3tog 4 times. Leaving a 12" yarn tail, cut yarn and draw end through 4 remaining loops.

Finishing

Assemble each unit (follow diagrams for cube and pyramid, matching points A to A, B to B, etc.). Sew flat seams, stuffing each object with the yarn tails and other yarn scraps as needed. Cut two 12" sections from dowel and spray paint them black. When the dowels are dry, cross them as shown and tie them securely at the center, wrapping and tying one end of a 40" piece of fishing line or yarn around the dowels to hold them in position, leaving the other end free to hang the mobile. Cut four 20" lengths of fishing line or yarn and tie each to an end of the dowels. Thread fishing line or yarn in tapestry needle and attach each object, adjusting length of line to 12."

RATTLE

Make 2 spheres and 1 rod. Insert a jingle bell into each sphere if you like.

Attach 1 sphere to each end of assembled rod.

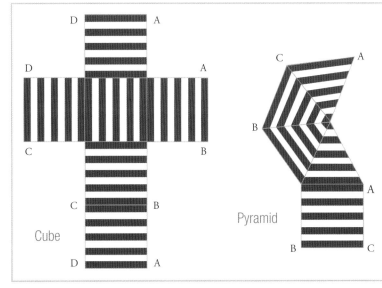

Cube

Pyramid

Bunny Bonnet and Stay-On Booties

Who can resist the quirky charm of bunny ears? These are so quick to make you may even finish the set in an evening or two. The bonnet is shaped with short-rows, a technique of working only some of the stitches on the needle. It enables you to increase or decrease the number of stitches and in effect creat a dart that does not require a seam. The heels of socks are often shaped with short rows, and this project offers a fun way to practice the technique. On the bonnet, you work from the front edge to the back, using the short row technique to decrease in two places simultaneously.

Each ear is worked in two pieces, seamed, and then stitched in place. Make an extra set of bunny ears following the Cuddly Bunny directions on page 108 if you want ears on the booties too. By doubling worsted weight yarn or working one strand of bulky yarn, you can make these stay-on booties to coordinate with any of the projects in the book.

Sizes

For bonnet and booties: 3-6 months (6-12 months, 12-18 months)

Materials

Needles: For bonnet, 16"-long circular needle size 9 (5.5mm); and 1 set of 4 double-pointed needles size 9 (5.5mm); for booties, one set of 4 double-pointed needles size 7 (4.5mm); or sizes needed to obtain correct gauge

Yarn: Cascade Yarns, 1 (2, 2) skeins of Bulky Leisure #8400 (Charcoal) for color A and small amount of Bulky Leisure #8010 (Ecru) for color B

Gauge

14 sts = 4" in stockinette st on larger needles

BONNET

Starting at front edge with circular needle and color A, cast on 39 (42, 45) sts, leaving a 4" yarn tail. Working back and forth on circular needle, knit 6 rows. Work 3½" (4", 4½") in stockinette st, knitting first and last st of every row for garter stitch edge.

Begin short row shaping for crown on next RS row: K25 (27, 29) sts, ssk, turn.

Next row (WS): P12 (13, 14), p2tog, turn.

Following row: K12 (13,14) sts, ssk, turn.

Next row: Repeat WS row.

Repeat these two rows 6 (7, 8) times more.

Bunny Bonnet

Nape shaping: Next row (RS): K1, ssk, k7 (8, 9), k2tog, ssk, turn.

Following row: P10 (11, 12) sts, p2tog, turn.

Next row: K1, ssk, k5 (6, 7), k2tog, ssk, turn.

Following row: P8 (9, 10) sts, p2tog, turn. Nape shaping is completed.

Continue decreasing at each turn until only the 9 (10, 11) sts of the middle third remain. Transfer these sts to a double-pointed needle (dpn) and cut yarn, leaving a short tail.

Neck border and ties

On circular needle, cast on and knit 17 (18, 19) sts for tie, then working onto same circular needle, pick up 11 (12, 13) sts evenly spaced along bottom of left side of bonnet (with RS of bonnet facing you), knit across the 9 (10, 11) sts of bonnet back (from dpn), pick up 11 (12, 13) sts along bottom of right side of bonnet, ending at front edge. Cast on and knit 17 (18, 19) sts for another tie at beginning of next row, knit to end [65 (70, 75) sts on needle].

Knit 4 rows even. Bind off loosely and weave in tails.

Ears

With color A and larger dpn and leaving a 12" yarn tail, cast on 12 sts. Knit 24 rows.

Shaping: K2tog at beg of next 8 rows. Knit 4 rows. K2tog at beg of next 3 rows. Bind off. Make two ears.

Ear lining

With color B and larger dpn and leaving a 12" yarn tail, cast on 12 sts. Knitting first and last st of every row for a garter stitch border, work 20 rows in stockinette st. Decrease as for ears. Make two ear linings.

Finishing

Using flat seam, sew a lining to each ear. Fold edges of ear forward to meet at the middle; stitch edges in place. Place ears side-by-side; then stitch the adjacent edges together for 1" at bottom. Attach ear unit to top of bonnet where right angle forms. Weave in ends. Block lightly, if desired.

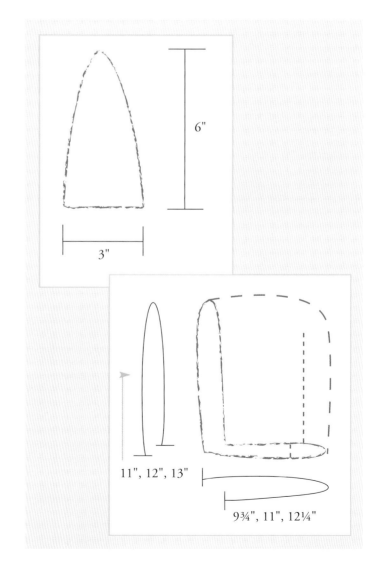

BOOTIES

Sole

With color A and smaller dpn needles and leaving a 4" yarn tail, cast on 5 sts. Working back and forth, knit 2 rows. Inc 1 st at beg of next 2 (4, 6) rows [7 (9, 11) sts on needle]. Work 22 (24, 26) rows even. Dec 1 st at beg of next 2 (4, 6) rows (5 sts).

Top

Next row (RS): K1, place first marker, k3 sts for toe, place second marker, k1, pick up 13 (15, 17) sts along left side of sole, pick up 5 from cast-on edge, pick up 13 (15, 17) sts along right side of sole and join for working in the round [36 (40, 44 sts) on needle].

Rnd 1: Knit.

Rnd 2: K3, slip second marker, ssk, knit to last 2 sts before first marker, k2tog.

Repeat these two rnds 3 (4, 5) more times.

Repeat rnd 2 only twice more, [24 (26, 28) sts on needle].

Finishing

I-cord edging: Knit to center back and cast on 3 sts. Begin knitting I-cord around edge of bootie as follows: K2, then working last I-cord st together with 1st from bootie, ssk. Slide work back to beg of row without turning. Continue in this manner until all bootie sts have been worked. Work 7 rows of I-cord on remaining 3 sts. Bind off. Stitch end to cast-on edge to form a loop as shown. Weave in ends. Make two booties.

Block lightly, if desired.

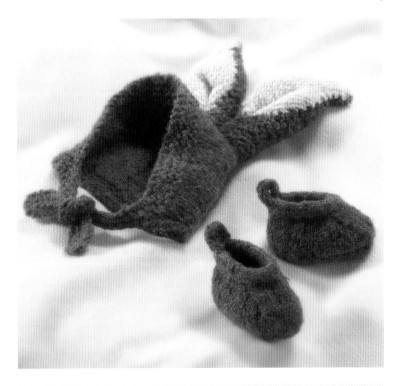

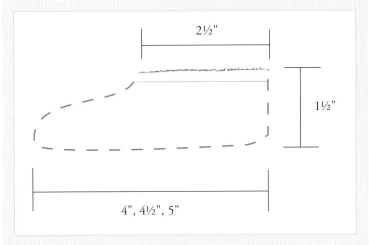

Cuddly Bunny

The bunny is based on the black and white mobile on page 101. With simple shapes and a little imagination you can make dolls, bears, pigs, sheep, cows, etc. The cotton/alpaca blend I've used is ideal for such projects since the fuzzy texture makes the construction forgiving. Facial features should always be embroidered (no button eyes). Using the photo as a guide, work satin stitch for the nose and eyes, and backstitch for the mouth (page 52). In a world filled with plastic toys, what could be more welcome than a soft handmade animal friend?

Size
Bunny is about 12" tall.

Materials
Needles: 1 set of 4 double-pointed needles in size 9 (5.5mm) or the size needed to obtain correct gauge.

Yarn: Cascade Yarns, 1 skein of Bulky Leisure #8400 (Charcoal)

Notions: Small quantities of pink, green, and black worsted weight yarn; tapestry needle

Gauge
14 sts = 4" in stockinette st

BUNNY

Head
Leaving a 12" yarn tail, work as for Sphere on page 101, substituting stockinette st for garter stitch, but knitting the first and last stitches on WS rows for a garter stitch edge.

Body
Leaving a 12" yarn tail, work as for head, working even in middle stockinette st portion for a total of 16 rows.

Arms
Leaving a 12" yarn tail, cast on 5 sts.

Row 1: Knit.

Row 2 and all even-numbered rows: K1, purl to last st, k1.

Row 3: *Bar inc (K in front and back of st); rep from * 3 times more, end k1 (9 sts on needle).

Work 14 rows in stockinette st, keeping garter stitch border. Bind off. Make two arms.

Legs
Leaving a 12" yarn tail, cast on 5 sts.

Row 1: Knit.

Row 2 and all even-numbered rows: K1, purl to last st, k1.

Row 3: *Bar inc; rep from * 3 times more, end k1, (9 sts on needle).

Row 5: Bar inc, knit to last st, bar inc (11 sts).

Cuddly Bunny

Work even in stockinette st for 12 rows, keeping garter
stitch border. Bind off. Make two legs.

Ears

Leaving a 12" yarn tail, cast on 7 sts.

Knit 14 rows. K2tog at beg of next 4 rows. Knit 2 rows.
Then k2tog at beg of every row until 1 st remains. Cut
yarn and draw through st.

Tail

Make a 12" pompon.

Blocking unnecessary.

Finishing

Blocking is unnecessary. Stuff bunny with yarn scraps
or other filling before closing head and body with flat
seams, tightly drawing the cast on and bound off
edges together. Sew arm and leg seams, starting from
the paws (cast-on edge). Stuff and attach them to
body. Attach head and tail to body. On ears, fold edges
to middle and sew in place; sew ears to head.
Embroider face (see page 50) as shown in photo,
using yarn colors as indicated. Buttons should not be
used for eyes unless intended for a much older child
or an adult recipient. Also be sure the whiskers are
knotted securely in place, to prevent them from being
pulled loose.

Feather and Fan
Crib Blanket

Feather and Fan Crib Blanket
(See next page for instructions)

Feather and Fan is an ancient Shetland Isle pattern with many names and variations, including old shale or shell, crest of the wave, and ostrich plumes. In my variation, (shown on page 111) the pattern row is worked every 6th row instead of the usual every 4th row. You could insert more rows of garter stitch without flattening the scallops. You could also work the pattern entirely in stockinette for a smooth fabric. Unlike most lace patterns where the decreases are paired with the yarn overs, here the decreases are grouped together, which forces the fabric ends into deep scallops.

Practice the pattern over a single repeat before jumping into the whole afghan. Then use markers between each repeat to keep your pattern on track. For a graceful, lacy shawl, use very fine yarn on size 8, 9, or 10 (5-6mm) needles. About 800-1000 yards will be enough to make your shawl 60" or larger.

Size

About 26" wide by 30" long.

Materials

Needles: 24"-long circular needles size 6 (4mm) and size 8 (5mm), or sizes needed to obtain correct gauge; straight needle size 10½ (6.5mm) for binding off

Yarn: Cascade Yarns, 3 skeins of 220 Superwash #5820 (Lemon)

Gauge

18 sts = 4" on larger needle in stockinette stitch

Stitch pattern

Multiple of 18 sts

Rows 1 and 5 (RS): Knit.

Rows 2 and 6: K3, purl to last 3 sts, k3.

Row 3: K3, (k2tog) 3 times, (yo, k1) 6 times, (k2tog) 3 times; repeat from *, end k3.

Row 4: Knit.

Repeat rows 1 through 6 for pattern

AFGHAN

With smaller needle and leaving a 7" tail, cast on 96 sts.

Work 6 rows garter stitch (knit every row). Change to larger needle and work 30 repeats of stitch pattern. Change to smaller needle and work 6 rows garter stitch. Bind off loosely, using larger needle if needed. Weave in yarn tails.

Block lightly, if desired.

Purple Crush Top-Down Pullover

The knit-from-the-top-down sweater method is perfect for fast-growing children because the sleeves and body can be picked up and lengthened repeatedly, until the body is too snug. I didn't invent this method; it's been around for a long time. It is possible that the first top-down was knit more than 700 years ago.

My students love the top-down sweater since it requires few if any seams. I prefer to knit sleeves flat and then sew the underarm seam to working in the round on double-pointed needles, but you might enjoy the novelty of a truly seamless sweater. Because you can try the sweater on as you go, this method is infinitely adaptable. It is possible, though not necessarily advisable, to dispense with all counting and measuring. Once you set up your increases with the aid of a marker at the front and back of each shoulder, there's no need to count. Increase once before and after each marker on every other round. The first few inches will require your full attention while you learn the rhythm of the increases. The slanting stitches on each raglan increase line should mirror, so be certain you are working your increases correctly: knit to one stitch before marker, increase, knit one, slip marker, knit one, increase. Don't make this common error: Increase, knit one, slip marker, increase, knit one. Because there are four markers, try this trick to designate the beginning of your round: use a red and a green safety-pin style marker, clipped together. At the beginning of an increase row slip the green marker. Switch to the red marker at the beginning of the plain round. I associate the green with "go" as in "go increase" and red with "stop" as in "stop increasing."

There are two color-pattern choices for this sweater: the vivid Purple Crush shown on the child on page 115 and the muted Lichen Stripe in the swatch. To create your own color-pattern from your yarn stash, cast on from 12 to 16 sts and knit a "test run" to try out various combinations. If you are purchasing new yarns, lay the selected skeins side by side to see if the colors are compatible. Be sure the yarns are also compatible for gauge and laundering.

If you follow this same pattern at a gauge of 3–3.5 stitches to the inch, you can make **an adult-sized sweater,** adjusting length of sleeves and body as needed to fit. Be sure to purchase enough additional yarn. I recommend that you take the time to do a fitting before separating the sleeves. Slip your stitches to yarn holders (see page 00), being sure to spread them out so you can see the full size--you might be surprised to find that it is a square. The corners should meet under the arms when you try it on so you'll see if it

actually fits, especially when your arms are extended forward. [ILL 44] Or lay it against an existing garment to see if the armhole is long enough and the body wide enough. Then, work each sleeve separately and join the front and back stitches to form the body. With a fitting, you can skip counting and measuring, but they provide an excellent double-check for estimating size. Count the stitches on the of back, multiply by two, and then divide by your gauge to determine body width.

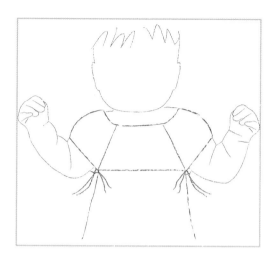

Sizes

3-6 months (6-12 months, 12-18 months)
Note: the garment shown is the 6-12 months size.

Materials

Needles: 16"-long circular needles size 7 (4.5mm) and size 9 (5.5mm); pairs of straight needles size 7 (4.5mm) and size 9 (5.5mm) for sleeves, or sizes needed to obtain correct gauge; straight needle size 11 (8mm) for binding off

Yarn: Cascade Yarns, 1 skein each as listed below:

Purple Stripe Colorway

Col.	Yarn	Col. #	Color Name	Col.
A	220 Tweed	#5610	Purple	Dk. Purple
B	220 Quatro	#9462	Cabernet Heather	Dk. Wine
C	220 Quatro	#9437	Malta	Med. Multi
D	220	#7809	Violet	Lt. Lavender
E	220 Superwash	#805	Violet	Med. Purple

Lichen Stripe Variation

Col.	Yarn	Col. #	Color Name	Col.
A	220 Tweed	#602	Evergreen	Dk. Green
B	220 Tweed	#619	Jet	Dk. Grey
C	220 Quatro	#9402	Dk. and Med. Grey Tweed	Med. Grey
D	220	#8401	Silver Grey	Lt. Grey
E	220	#9460	Dune Heather	Lt. Green

Gauge

16 sts and 26 rows = 4" in stockinette st on larger needles

Purple Crush
Top-Down
Pullover with
color variation

Stripe pattern

Neck Facing and Yoke		Sleeves and Body	
D:	8 (8, 10) rows/rounds	**E:**	4 (4, 6)
C:	10 (10, 10)	**D:**	1 (1, 1)
B:	5 (6, 6)	**E:**	2 (3, 3)
A:	2 (2, 2)	**B:**	1 (2, 2)
B:	2 (2, 2)	**A:**	2 (2, 2)
A:	3 (4, 4)	**B:**	2 (2, 4)
E:	1 (1,1)	**E:**	4 (4, 4)
A:	3 (5, 5)	**C:**	2 (2, 4)
D:	3 (5, 5)	**D:**	4 (4, 6)
C:	1 (1, 1)	**C:**	8 (8, 8)
D:	2 (2, 3)	**D:**	7 (7, 7)
C:	2 (2, 2)	**Subtotal:** 37 (39, 47)	
E:	1 (1, 1)	rows/rnds	
C:	2 (2, 2)		
D:	1 (1, 1)		
E:	2 (2, 2)		
C:	1 (1, 1)		
Subtotal: 49 (55, 58) rows/rnds			

PULLOVER

Note: Refer to the stripe pattern above for the color sequence and number of rows or rounds of each color to knit for each size. You begin with a neck facing and end with hem facings, these are not visible in the photo. At each color change, knit the first stitch of the round with both the old and the new yarns held together (see page 35).

Neck facing

Row 1: With color D and smaller circular needles and leaving a 12" yarn tail, cast on 60 sts for all sizes. Join and knit 7 (7, 9) rnds.

Yoke

Change to color C and purl 1 rnd. Change to larger needles and begin increasing at the rate of 8 sts every other rnd using the lifted method (see page 38) as follows: * Place marker onto right needle (M), k1, inc, k13, inc, k1; repeat from * three more times (68 sts on needle). Your work is now separated into four identical sections, corresponding to the right sleeve, front, left sleeve, and back.

Next rnd: Knit, slipping the markers.

Continue increasing one st each side of each marker every other rnd, working 7 more rnds in color C and then continuing in stripe pattern at left until you have 172 (188, 204) sts on needle.

Divide for sleeves

At beg of next rnd, slip marker, k43 (47, 51) right sleeve sts (up to 2nd marker) onto pair of larger straight needles. Now work back and forth in stockinette st over just the sleeve sts while the rest of the sweater waits on the circular needle as a holder. Continuing with stripe pattern, work even for 3 (5, 9) more rows.

Decrease row (RS): K2, ssk, knit to last 4 sts, k2tog, k2. Repeat this row every 4th row until 31 (33, 33) sts remain.

Change to smaller straight needles and continue stripe pattern through 7 rows of last repeat of Color C. Then, with Color C, purl 1 row. Change to color D. Knit 7 rows. Bind off loosely with largest needles, leaving an 18" yarn tail.

Join yarn to sts on circular needle (RS row, beg of front), work across 43 (47, 51) front sts, then work 43 (47, 51) left sleeve sts onto larger straight needles; complete sleeve as for right sleeve, leaving front and back sts on circular needle.

Body

Join yarn to sts on circular needle at beg of back (RS row). Knit across back sts to complete rnd. Then,

joining body at underarms, work 22 (24, 32) rnds in stripe pattern. Change to smaller needles and work 7 more rnds with Color C. Purl 1 rnd. Change to color D and knit 7 rnds. Bind off loosely, with largest needle.

Finishing

Turn under neck, bottom and sleeve hems along purl stitch ridge and whip-stitch in place. Weave in yarn tails.

Block lightly, if desired.

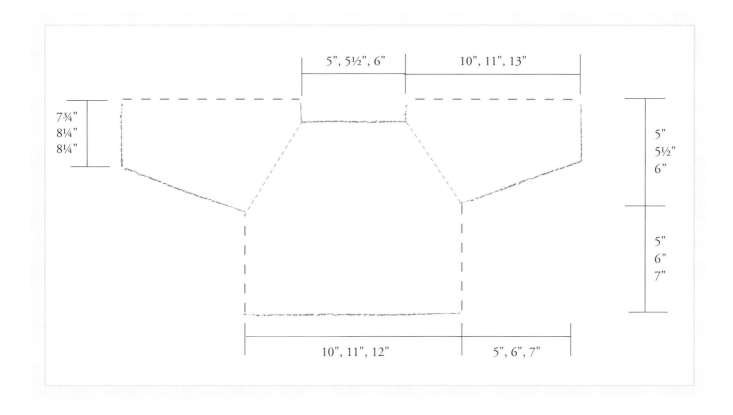

Seeds and Vines
Top-Down Cardigan

This cardigan illustrates just how versatile from-the-top-down knitting can be. By placing more stitches in the middle of each raglan increase, you can add a narrow cable or lace pattern. Here the cables are twisted more tightly than usual to resemble vines. Seed stitch edging complements the botanical theme and is easy to work. Use markers and remember to always work the seed stitch areas k1, p1, k1, p1, k1 no matter which side is facing you. The yarn overs are employed as both an increase method and a decorative detail, setting off the cables without the use of purl stitches. Waist shaping adds a graceful touch to this classic garment. To make an adult version, work the smallest size at a gauge of 4 stitches to the inch. Work the yoke for about 9-10" and until you have enough stitches for desired width (36"–38" for a woman's medium and 42"–44" for a man's medium). Regardless of what size you are making, the best way to determine the correct length for the yoke and the width for the body is to take those measurements from an existing, well-fitting garment.

Sizes
3-6 months (6-12 months, 12-18 months)

Materials
Needles: 16"- or 24"-long circular needles size 5 (3.75mm) and size 7 (4.5mm), pairs of straight needles size 5 (3.75mm) and size 7 (4.5mm) for sleeves, or sizes needed to obtain correct gauge; cable needle, straight needle size 10½ (6.5mm) for binding off.

Yarn: Cascade Yarns, 2 (3, 3) skeins of "220" #7814 (Lime Heather)

Notions: Five ⅝"-diameter buttons

Gauge
22 sts and 30 rows = 4" in stockinette st on larger needles

Cable stitch pattern
(Worked on 6 sts)

Row 1: Knit.

Rows 2 and 4: Purl.

Row 3: Slip 3 sts to cable needle and hold in front of work, k3, k3 st from cable needle (3-by-3 FC).

Seeds and Vines Top-Down Cardigan

CARDIGAN

Yoke

With larger circular needle and leaving a 12" yarn tail, cast on 64 (74, 84) sts. Do not join sts, but work back and forth on circular needle.

Row 1: Establish raglan sections and begin increasing at the rate of 8 sts on this and then every following RS row as follows:

K1, P1, K1, P1, K1 (seed 5), k5 (7, 9), yo, place marker on needle (M), k6, (M), yo (left front); K4 (6, 8), yo, (M), k6, (M), yo (left sleeve); K12 (14, 16), yo, (M), k6, (M), yo (back); K4 (6, 8), yo, (M), k6, (M), yo (right sleeve); K5 (7, 9), seed 5 (right front). Turn work.

Row 2 (WS): Slipping markers and working the yarn overs made on previous row as stitches, seed 5, purl to last 5 sts, seed 5.

Row 3 (RS): Seed 5, knit to next marker, yo, slip M, work cable stitch pattern row 3 on next 6 sts, slip M, yo; repeat from * 3 times more, knit to last 5 sts, seed 5.

Repeat these last 2 rows (but cross the cable every other RS row), 16 (18, 20) more times, or until you have 200 (218, 236) sts on needle AND AT THE SAME TIME work a buttonhole every 16th (18th, 20th) row as follows: for girls, at end of RS rows (on right front seed st border) K1, yo, k2tog, p1, k1. For boys, (at beg of RS rows on left front) K1, p1, k2tog, yo, k1.

Divide for sleeves: Note: As you divide the work, each set of 6 cable stitches will be split, with 3 stitches going to each adjacent section. Remove markers. Continue to work buttonholes (a total of 4 for all sizes);

the 5th (top) buttonhole will be worked on the first row of neckband.

At beg of next RS row, k30 (34, 38) left front sts. K44 (50, 56) left sleeve sts onto pair of larger straight needles. Now work back and forth over just the sleeve sts while the rest wait on the circular needle as holder. Work even for 5 (11, 17) more rows.

Decrease row (RS): K2, ssk, knit to last 4 sts, k2tog, k2. Repeat this row every 4th row until you have 32 (34, 34) sts on needle.

Change to smaller straight needles and decrease 1 st at beg of next RS row: K1, p1, ssk, *p1, k1; rep from *. Work 4 more rows in seed stitch. Bind off in seed stitch with largest needle if needed. Leave an 18" yarn tail.

Join yarn to sts on circular needle (RS row, at beg of back), work across 52 (58, 64) back sts: Change to larger straight needles and continue across 44 (50, 56) right sleeve sts; complete sleeve as for left sleeve.

Body

Join yarn to sts on circular needle at underarm edge of right front (RS row) and knit across row, end seed 5. Turn, seed 5, purl across right front, place marker onto right needle (M), purl across back sts, (M), purl across left front to last 5 sts, seed 5 [112 (126, 140) sts total]. Keeping borders in seed st, work even in stockinette st for 6 (8, 10) more rows, ending on a WS row.

Decrease row (RS): Seed 5, *knit to 2 sts before M,

k2tog, slip M, ssk; repeat from * once more, knit to last 5 sts, seed 5. Repeat dec every 8th row 2 more times. Work even for 4 (4, 6) more rows; dec 1 on last row to make an uneven number of sts for seed st bottom border. Change to smaller circular needle and work 4 rows in seed st. Bind off loosely in seed stitch with largest needles if needed.

Finishing

Neck band: With smaller circular needle, leaving a 24" tail, and starting at right front neck edge with RS facing you, pick up 63 (71, 79) sts AND AT THE SAME TIME, work final buttonhole on pick-up row as follows: Pick up 3 sts, skip 2, continue row.

Next row: Working in seed stitch, cast on 2 sts in skipped space on previous row. Work 6 more rows in seed stitch. Bind off loosely in seed stitch.

Starting at cuff edge, sew sleeve seams. With sewing thread, sew buttons to front border opposite buttonholes. Weave in yarn tails.

Block lightly, if desired.

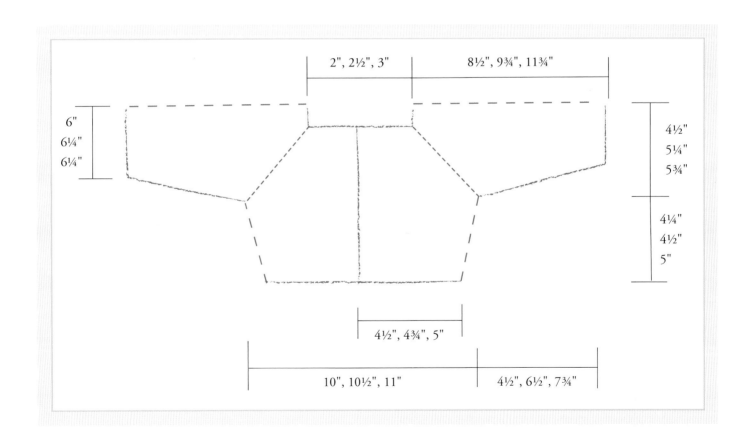

Ribbon-Tied Round-Yoke Sacque

An instant heirloom, this is the simplest top-down garment I teach. At 6 stitches to the inch, it has the finest gauge of all the projects in this book. Our ancestors often knitted at gauges from 12 to 28 stitches to the inch. Larger stitch sizes didn't become a trend until the industrial revolution and the advent of advertising and mass production. Many new knitters prefer working on a large gauge to complete projects in the shortest possible time. But aside from developing your patience, there are several other reasons to try finer needles and yarn. The thinner the yarn is spun the more fabric it can make, so it's more economical, a consideration of considerable importance to our knitting ancestors for whom materials were often scarce. (Historically, the richest periods in the development of techniques and patterns have occurred at times and places where there was a chronic shortage of materials.) Scale is another reason: Babies are small, so smaller stitches are appropriate for the dainty proportions of tiny features. Thinner needles are also easier to manipulate, allowing you to increase your speed effortlessly. Although it takes more stitches to make an inch, you can knit those stitches much faster.

The ribbons threaded through the eyelets on the yoke and cuffs of the sacque are functional as well as decorative, gently gathering the fabric and tying the garment closed. You'll be delighted by how little attention this fancy-looking classic requires.

Sizes

3-6 months (6-12 months, 12-18 months)

Materials

Needles: 16"- or 24"-long circular needle size 6 (4mm), 1 pair straight needles size 6 (4mm) for sleeves, or size needed to obtain correct gauge; straight needle size 8 (5mm) for binding off

Yarn: Cascade Yarns, 2 (2, 3) skeins of Cherub DK #5002 (French Vanilla)

Notions: 6 yards ¼"-wide velvet ribbon

Gauge

24 sts = 4" in stockinette stitch

Ribbon-Tied Round-Yoke Sacque

starting a knitting circle

A weekly or monthly knitting circle is an invaluable resource and offers a wonderful way to socialize and be productive. Knitters living in rural areas can rely on an extensive community on the Internet (page 140). Join an existing group or start your own. You don't need a lot of experience or technical knowledge to create a supportive environment, just enthusiasm, a place to meet, and a few friends who knit or want to learn. Ideally, have at least one member who can demonstrate the basics. If everyone is a complete beginner you can work through The Course in Part I together.

Or you might want to hire a private teacher to give a group lesson to get you started. If you live in a city and want to recruit a dynamic group, schedule your meetings at a quiet café and you will attract curious onlookers.

Ask veteran knitters in your group or among your friends to give special workshops on their specialties. Encourage members of all levels to share what they know and create a hothouse environment where everyone exceeds her expectations. And charitable projects go quickly when done by a group.

SACQUE

Yoke

With circular needle and leaving a 7" yarn tail, cast on 54 (62, 70) sts. Do not join sts, but work back and forth on circular needle.

Rows 1 through 4: Knit.

Row 5 (RS): K3, *yo, k2tog; rep from *, end k3 (eyelet row made).

Rows 6: Knit, working each yo loop as one st.

Rows 7 through 11: Work in stockinette st, keeping first 3 and last 3 sts in garter stitch.

Rows 12 and 14 (WS): Knit.

Row 13 (eyelet row): K3, *yo, k1; repeat from *, end k3 [101 (117, 133) sts on needle].

Rows 15 through 19: Work in stockinette st, keeping first 3 and last 3 sts in garter stitch.

Row 20 (WS): Knit.

Row 21: Repeat row 13 [194 (227, 259) sts].

Work in stockinette st (always keeping first 3 and last 3 sts in garter stitch) until work measures 5½" (6½", 7½") from cast-on edge.

Left sleeve

On next RS row, work across 27 (32, 37) sts (for left front), then with straight size 6 needle, knit across 45 (51, 57) sts (for left sleeve), leaving remaining sts on circular needle. Working on sleeve sts only, work even in stockinette st for 1½".

Continuing in stockinette st, decrease every 4th row (on RS) as follows: K2, ssk, knit to last 4 sts, k2tog, k2, until 33 (35, 37) sts remain.

Next row (WS): Knit.

Following row (eyelet row): K1, *yo, k2tog; rep from *, end k2.

Knit 3 rows and bind off loosely, with larger needle if needed.

Right sleeve

Join yarn to sts on circular needle (RS row, at beg of back), and k50 (61, 71) sts, then on straight needle, k45 (51, 57) sts for right sleeve; complete sleeve as for left sleeve.

Body

Join yarn to sts on circular needle at underarm edge of right front (RS row) and work across as established.

Joining row (WS): K3, purl right front sts, continue across back and then left front sts, end k3 [108 (128, 148) sts total].

Work in stockinette (keeping first 3 and last 3 sts at front edges in garter stitch) until work measures 9½" (10½", 11½") from cast-on edge, ending with a WS row.

Eyelet row: K2, * yo, k2tog; rep from *, end k2. Knit 3 rows. Bind off loosely, with larger needle if necessary.

Finishing

Sew sleeve seams using mattress stitch. Weave in yarn tails. Thread ribbon through each eyelet row, adjust tension and then trim ends. You can omit the ribbon ties and fasten with three buttons; the eyelet holes make buttonholes unnecessary.

Block lightly, if desired.

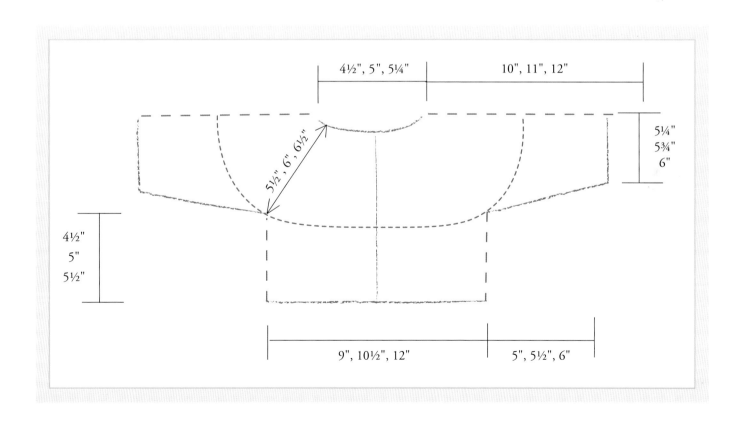

Heirloom Aran Sweater and Accessories

Aran sweaters display a rich tradition of cable and other texture patterns that developed in the Aran Islands, off the coast of Ireland. Many of these patterns have nautical themes (ropes, anchors, waves) or natural themes (seeds, moss, berries, trees). To work a cable, simply knit the stitches out of order. By slipping one or more stitches to an extra needle and holding it aside while you knit the next few stitches, the stitches overlap, or cable around each other. Each family of Aran knitters created its own arrangement of the many traditional patterns, akin to Scottish kilts as clan identifiers. This is the smallest version of my family Aran pattern. Without changing scale, it distills the essence of a more complex arrangement of patterns.

What does your family Aran look like? Like me, you may have to design your own. Did your great-aunt have a favorite cable stitch pattern? Ask older family members if they have any heirloom hand-knits you can plunder for inspiration. Barbara Walker's first and second *Treasury of Knitting Patterns* (see page 140) are an excellent source of stitch patterns with thorough instructions on how to design your own Aran.

For this sweater, the shaping and garment structure are deliberately simple so you can focus on the textures. The shoulders are joined with the three-needle bind off, the sleeves are picked up and worked from the armhole to the cuff. The wide neck precludes a button closure. The folded-over neckband takes the stress off the bound-off edge.

Consider experimenting with color. Undyed, off-white sheep's wool is the traditional choice. Green, grey, red, and blue are other favorites of mine. Pink, yellow, or orange would be dynamic and fun to work. A word of advice: Until you are confident working with assorted patterns, avoid dark colors—it is much easier to see your work in a lighter color.

Sizes

3-6 months (12-18 months)

Materials

Needles: 16"-long circular needles size 5 (3.75mm) and size 8 (5mm), or sizes needed to obtain correct gauge; cable needle; crochet hook size G (5mm) for mitten cord, straight needle size 10 (6mm) for binding off (optional)

Yarns: Cascade Yarns, 1 skein of Eco Wool #8010 (Ecru)

Notions: One ⅝"-diameter button for hood; stitch holders

Heirloom Aran
Sweater

Working Multiple Patterns on Aran Sweaters

If you are a new knitter, you may think you could never knit anything so intricate as an Aran sweater. You can. The key is practicing each pattern separately until your fingers have "memorized" it. When you combine all the patterns, use markers to separate them and a row counter to keep track of your place in each. If you know which row of the sweater you are on, you will be able to know which row of an individual stitch pattern to work. For instance, if you are on the 12th row of the sweater (above ribbing), work the 2nd row of a pattern with a 10-row repeat (12 - 10 = 2), the 6th row of a 6-row repeat (12 - 6 = 6), the 4th row of an 8-row repeat (12 - 8 = 4), and so on.

Gauge

18 sts and 30 rows = 4" in stockinette st on larger needles

Stitch patterns

Pattern A (double seed stitch)

(Multiple of 2 sts)

Rows 1 and 2: *K1, p1; rep from *.

Rows 3 and 4: *P1, k1; rep from*.

Repeat rows 1 through 4 for pattern.

Pattern B (4-stitch cable, back cross)

(Multiple of 4 sts)

Row 1 (RS): Knit.

Rows 2 and 4: Purl.

Row 3: Slip 2 sts to cable needle and hold in back; k2, slip 2 sts on cable needle back to left needle, k2 (2-by-2, BC, completed).

Repeat rows 1 through 4 for pattern.

Pattern C (4-stitch cable, front cross)

(Multiple of 4 sts)

Row 1 (RS): Knit.

Rows 2 and 4: Purl.

Row 3: Slip 2 sts to cable needle and hold in front, k2, slip 2 sts on cable needle back to left needle, k2 (2-by-2 front cable, FC, completed). Repeat rows 1-4.

Pattern D (double-seed filled diamond)

Row 1 (RS): P5, work 2-by-2 FC (as on Row 3 of Pattern C, above), p5.

Row 2 and all WS rows: Knit the knit sts and purl the purl sts as they face you (see page 33).

Row 3: P4, then slip 1 st to cable needle and hold to back, K2, slip st from cable needle back to left needle, k1 (back knit cross, BKC), then slip 2 sts to cable needle and hold to front, p1, slip sts from cable needle back to left needle, k2 (front purl cross, FPC), p4.

Row 5: P3, BKC, p1, K1, FPC, p3.

Row 7: P2, BKC, work (p1, k1) twice, FPC, p2.

Row 9: P1, BKC, work (p1, k1) 3 times, FPC, p1.

Row 11: BKC, work (p1, k1) 4 times, FPC.

Row 13: K2, work (p1, k1) 5 times, k2.

Row 15: FPC, work (p1, k1) 4 times, slip 1 st to cable needle and hold in back of work, k2, slip st from cable needle onto left needle, p1, (back purl cross, BPC).

Row 17: P1, FPC, work (p1, k1) 3 times, BPC, p1.

Row 19: P2, FPC, work (p1, k1) twice, BPC, p2.

Row 21: P3, FPC, p1, k1, BPC, p3.

Row 23: P4, FPC, BPC, p4.

Row 24: Knit the knit sts and purl the purl sts as they face you.

Repeat rows 1 through 24 for pattern.

MITTENS

Right Mitten

With smaller needles and leaving a 4" yarn tail, cast on 31 sts. Work 1-by-1 rib for 1" (1½"). Change to larger needles for larger size mittens.

Establish pattern row 1 (RS): K1, work Pattern A over 12 sts, k1, p bar inc (p in front and back of st), work Pattern D over 14 sts, p bar inc, k1, (33 sts). Use markers to separate patterns.

Row 2 and all WS rows: K1, work in patterns as established and work the 3 stitches between patterns as they face you (knit the knit and purl the purl sts), end k1.

Row 3: K1, work Pattern A over 12 sts, k1, p2, work Pattern D over 14 sts, p2, k1.

Work even in patterns until row 14 is completed.

Row 15: K1, ssk, work Pattern A as established (see page 99) over 9 sts, k2tog, p2tog, work Pattern D over 12 sts, p2tog, k1 (29 sts).

Continue decreasing every other row in this manner until there are 14 sts left.

Next row: K1, SK2P, p2tog, work final 2 by 2 FC of Pattern D, p2tog, k1 (10 sts remain).

Cut yarn and draw through loops. Sew flat seam along side edges and weave in yarn ends.

Left Mitten

Cast on and work ribbing as for right mitten.

Establish pattern row (RS): K1, p bar inc, work Pattern D over 14 sts, p bar inc, k1, work Pattern A over 12

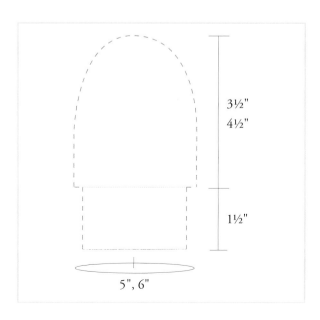

sts, k1 (33 sts). Complete to correspond to right mitten.

Finishing

Crochet a 24" (30") chain (see page 51) and attach an end to each mitten at seam at cuff edge. Weave in yarn tails.

HOOD

With larger needles cast on 60 (68) sts.

Establish pattern row 1 (RS): K1, work Pattern A over 9 (13) sts (end k1), k1, p2, work Pattern B twice over 8 sts, p2, work Pattern D over 14 sts, p2, work Pattern C twice over 8 sts, p2, k1, work Pattern A over 9 (13) sts (end k1), k1. Use markers to separate patterns.

Row 2 and all WS rows: K1, work in patterns as established, end k1.

Work as established until you have worked 32 (36) rows.

Begin short row shaping on next row (RS): Work 47 (51) sts in pattern, ssk, turn work without completing the row.

Next row (WS): K1, work in pattern as established across 28 sts, k2tog, turn.

Repeat these two rows until the middle third has "eaten up" the two outer thirds and 30 sts remain. Bind off.

Border: With smaller needles, leaving a 24" yarn tail, cast on 7 sts.

Row 1 (RS): K1, *k1, p1; rep from *, end k2.

Row 2: K1, *p1, k1; rep from *, end p1, k1.

Repeat these 2 rows and work even until piece measures 14" (16") or for 104 (120) rows. Bind off.

Make a second piece to match, ending with a WS row, but do not bind off. Work buttonhole on next row (RS): K2,

p2tog, yo, p1, k2. Starting with a row 2, work 3 more rows in pattern. Bind off.

Finishing

Using flat seam, stitch first border around face edge. Then stitch second border around neck edge starting with plain (cast-on) edge flush with left front border edge and the buttonhole end extending to pass under child's chin. Sew button in place on left edge. Weave in yarn tails.

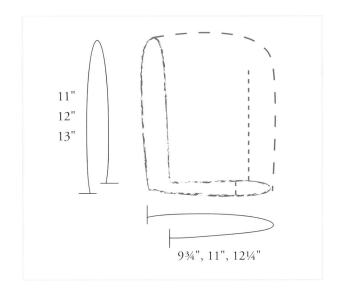

11"
12"
13"

9¾", 11", 12¼"

SWEATER

Back

With smaller needles and leaving a 24" yarn tail, cast on 55 (63) sts. Work 1-by-1 rib for 1½." Change to larger needles and continue as follows, placing markers to separate the patterns.

Establish pattern row 1: K1, work Pattern A over 8 (12) sts, k1, p bar inc, work Pattern B twice over 8 sts, p

Volunteer!

Knitting for others is a wonderful way to contribute to your community. There are many opportunities to volunteer on the Internet (page 140), or there may already be a local program for you to join. Whether you knit preemie clothes, cancer caps, hats for the homeless, or scarves for overseas soldiers, your contributions will be tangible messages of care.

Knitting can also function as a bridge between communities. If you have a relative living in an assisted care community consider setting up an exchange program with your grade-schooler's class to collaborate on a special project. Documenting the project with photos, drawings, and quotes lends a tremendous feeling of accomplishment and serves as a keepsake for all.

Knitting for charity is the perfect way to use up the odds and ends in your stash. If your program needs yarn, soliciting yarn donations is easy: Get the word out through your newsletter or phone tree and you will be amazed at what turns up. Yarn companies sometimes donate discontinued and imperfect yarn, so send a request and, if your timing is right, your program could acquire a jackpot of luxury yarn. And if you have unwanted yarn, donate it to another group.

---

bar inc (p in front and back of st), work Pattern D over 14 sts, p bar inc, work Pattern C twice over 8 sts, p2 (without increasing), k1, work Pattern A over 8 (12) sts, k1 [58 (66) sts total].

Row 2 and all WS rows: K1, work even in patterns as established, and work the 3 stitches between patterns as they face you (knit the knit and purl the purl sts), end k1.

Row 3: K1, work Pattern A over 8 (12) sts, k1, p2, work Pattern B twice over 8 sts, p2, work Pattern D over 14 sts, p2, work Pattern C twice over 8 sts, p2, k1, work Pattern A over 8 (12) sts, k1.

Work even in patterns until you have 2½ (3) repeats of Pattern D, or 60 (72) pattern rows above ribbing.

Place all sts on holder.

Front

Work as for back until you have 2 (2½) repeats of Pattern D, or 48 (60) pattern rows above ribbing; end with WS row.

Neck shaping: On next row (RS) work 38 (42) sts; place these stitches on a holder for left side while you finish the right side. Continuing on the remaining 20 (24) sts, bind off 1 (2) sts at neck edge every other row a total of 3 times. Work even over remaining 17 (18) sts for 4 more rows. Place these stitches on holder.

Leaving the center 18 sts on holder return the remaining 20 (24) sts left front sts to needle. Join yarn at neck edge on wrong side. Complete as for right side, decreasing at neck edge. Leaving center 24 (30) back neck sts on holder, join shoulders using three-needle bind off.

Sleeves

With safety pins, mark side edges of back and front 4½" (5½") from hem edge for armholes. With RS of work facing you, using smaller needles and leaving a 12" yarn tail, pick up 45 (53) sts evenly spaced between markers.

Next row (WS): Increase 13 sts across row as follows:

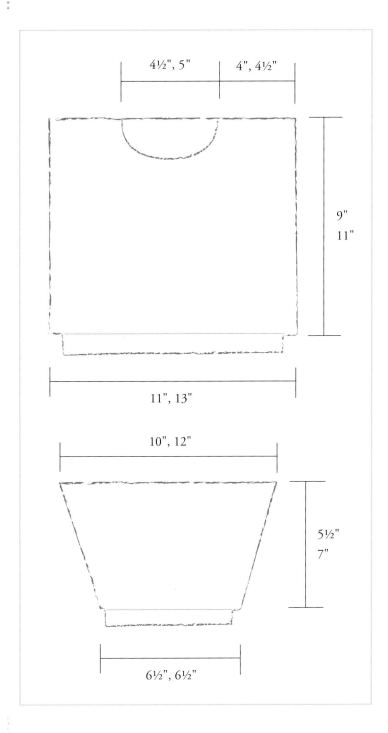

4½", 5"   4", 4½"

9"
11"

11", 13"

10", 12"

5½"
7"

6½", 6½"

Bar inc twice, work (k1, p1) 5 (7) times, bar inc, p bar inc, p2, bar inc twice, k3, p2, p bar inc, k3, bar inc twice, p2, p bar inc, bar inc, work (k1, p1) 5 (7) times, bar inc twice [58 (66) sts total].

Establish pattern row (RS): Change to larger needles. K1, work Pattern A over 12 (16) sts, k1, p2, work Pattern B over 4 sts, p2, work Pattern D over 14 sts, p2, work Pattern C over 4 sts, p2, k1, work Pattern A over 12 (6) sts, k1.

Work even in patterns as established until sleeve measures 2". Keeping continuity of patterns as established (see page 99), decrease 1 st at each end of every 4th row until 40 sts remain.

Change to smaller needles and decrease 9 sts across row as follows: K2tog, (p1, k1) twice, p2tog, k1, p1, k2tog, p2tog, (k1, p1) 6 times, k2tog, p2tog, k2tog, p2tog, (k1, p1) twice, k2tog (31 sts remain). Continue in 1-by-1 ribbing as now established for 1½". Bind off in ribbing.

Finishing

Neckband: With smaller needle, pick up 70 (78) sts around neck. Work in 1-by-1 ribbing for 2" (2½") and bind off loosely, with large needle if needed.

Fold neckband in half to inside. Whip stitch bound-off edge to inside at base of neckband.

Sew flat seams for sleeves and sides. Weave in yarn ends. Block lightly, if desired.

Country Patchwork Afghan

This final project is based on repetition and variation of a simple geometric shape. The triangle is a basic unit in traditional American patchwork, where there are countless patterns with an infinite number of possible arrangements. In this afghan, the blocks are squares formed of triangular halves worked in different colors. By starting at one corner of the square and increasing one stitch at the beginning of every row, you only need to keep track of your stitch count. When the triangle is wide enough, you change color, work 2 rows even, and then start decreasing by knitting two stitches together at the beginning of every row. At less than an hour per unit, you can realistically make one square block each day and complete the project in a month.

To simplify tracking the color combinations you have completed, use the "Road Trip Calculator," page 135, checking off each block as you knit it. When all 24 blocks are knitted, arrange them following the diagram on page 136. You might find it more satisfying to go "off road" and improvise the distribution and combinations of color. On page 136 are some examples of other ways to arrange groups of blocks.

Included in the sample as an accent is a wild card block composed of four smaller blocks, to serve as a suggestion for further experimentation. The change in scale adds depth to the afghan's surface. Work an extra block in the AC color combination if you would like to omit the more challenging wild card.

Several of the blocks feature leaf and bobble motifs. You may omit these motifs altogether for a simpler version. Knitters with more time to invest might like to work a motif in every square so that the leaves cluster together when assembled, for a contemporary version of the traditional Victorian counterpane. These fashionable bed-coverings were nearly always knit in white cotton on 1.5-2.0mm (U.S. #0000-#2) needles. Yours will be done in a fraction of the time on the much larger size 10½ needles.

Size

Each square unit measures about 5" square.
Afghan measures about 27" by 33" [outside dimensions]

Materials

Needles: 1 pair of straight needles size 10½ (6.5mm) for blocks, or size needed to obtain correct gauge; 36"-long circular needle size 10½ (6.5mm) for border

Country Patchwork Afghan

Yarns: Cascade yarns, 1 skein of Pastaza in each of the following colors:

Color A:	#078	(Wheat)
Color B:	#041	(Turmeric)
Color C:	#077	(Birch)
Color D:	#042	(Granny Smith)
Color E:	#069	(Lime Heather)
Color F:	#085	(Summer Sky Heather)
Color G:	#003	(Poppy)

Gauge

14 sts = 4" in stockinette st

Road Trip Calculator

To read the road trip calculator, pick a color from the left hand column and read across the row to find color pairings. For example, Block #14 is half Color A and half Color B. It doesn't matter which color you start with except when making the bobble leaf units, which are formed with the second color. The parentheses indicate where to work the motifs. Coordinates AE and DE both are worked twice, once with and once without the bobble leaf motif. (Block #11, the wild card variation, is not on the chart; see page 136 to make it.)

	A	B	C	D	E	F	G
A		14	17	2 (A)	19 (E)	1	3
					24		
B			18 (C)	9	15	13	8 (B)
C				23	12	6	21
D					16 (D)	5	20
					22		
E						10 (F)	7
F							4 (G)

AFGHAN

Basic Block

Starting at one corner and leaving an 18" yarn tail, cast on 3 sts. Knit 1 row. Work in garter stitch (knit every row) and inc 1 st (using bar method) at beginning of each row for 22 rows (25 sts).

Change color and knit 2 rows even.

K2tog at beg of next 21 rows (4 sts remain).

Last row (WS): Bind off remaining sts, beginning with k2tog.

Bobble leaf variation

Note: The leaf is created by increases that balance the block edge decreases so you have 25 sts on the needle until you begin decreasing the leaf sts. As you work, slip each marker from left to right needle.

Leaving an 18" tail, cast on 3 sts. Knit 1 row.

Work as for basic block until you have 25 sts.

Row 24: Change color and k12, work bobble in next stitch as follows: K1, yo, k1, yo, k1, turn work; p5, turn; k5, turn; p2tog, k1, p2tog, turn; slip 1, k2tog, PSSO (bobble completed and stitch count restored); k12 (25 sts).

Row 25: K12, place marker (M), p1, place marker, k12.

Row 26 (RS): K2tog, knit to M, yo, K1, yo, M, knit to end.

Wrong-side rows: K2tog, knit to M, purl to M, knit to end.

Row 28: K2tog, knit to M, k1, yo, k1, yo, k1, M, knit to end.

Row 30: K2tog, knit to M, k2, yo, k1, yo, k2, M, knit to end.

Row 32: K2tog, knit to M, k3, yo, k1, yo, k3, M, knit to end.

Row 34: K2tog, knit to M, k4, yo, k1, yo, k4, M, knit to end.

Rows 36, 38, 40 and 42: K2tog, k to M, ssk, knit to 2 sts before M, k2tog, M, k to end.

Row 44: K2tog, knit to M, slip 1, k2tog, PSSO (double decrease), M, knit to end.

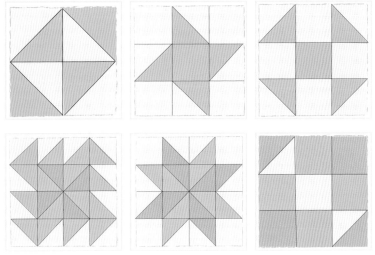

Row 46: Knit.

Row 47: K2tog. Bind off remaining sts.

Block #11: Wild Card variations

Sub Block 1: With Color C, cast on 3 sts and work as for basic block until you have 11 sts. Do not change color, decrease as for basic block.

Sub Block 2: With Color F, cast on 3 sts and work as for basic block until you have 11 sts. Change to Color E and decrease as for basic block. Note: in the sample, this block is deliberately reversed to show the intersection of the two colors that occurs on the "wrong" side of garter stitch.

Sub Block 3: With Color D, cast on 3 sts and work as for basic block until you have 11 sts. Change to Color F, k5, work bobble in next st as for bobble leaf variation, k5. Decrease as for basic block (omit leaf).

Sub Block 4: With Color B, cast on 3 sts and work as for basic block until you have 11 sts. Change to Color G and work bobble and mini leaf as follows: K5, work bobble in next st, k5.

Continue following rows 25 through 30 for bobble leaf variation, working only 5 sts outside the markers. To decrease, follow rows 36 and 44.

Finishing

Lay out squares, following assembly diagram at lower left. Join squares, sewing flat seams. Weave in all yarn tails.

Block lightly, if desired.

Borders

Following the diagram and using circular needle and first yarn color (see list below), pick up 14 stitches (1 in each trough) along each free edge of each block to pick up the total number of sts indicated for each section. Knit each section separately as follows: Knit 1 rnd. Change to second color and knit 2 rnds. Bind off loosely. When all sections are complete, sew their edges together. Weave in yarn tails.

Left border: C, B, (84 sts).
Bottom border: F, A, (98 sts).
Right border: E, D, (84 sts).
Top border: G, A, (98 sts).

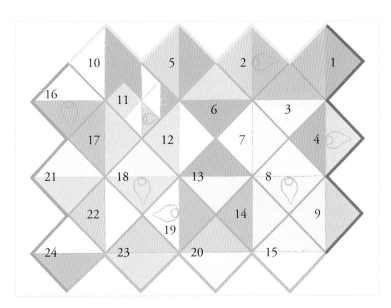

Appendices

Appendix A: Abbreviations and Terms

Abbreviation	Definition
BC	back cross (knit all stitches)
BO	bind off
BPC	back purl cable (knit the first stitches, purl the cabled stitches)
bar inc	knit into front, then back of same stitch to increase
beg	beginning
bet	between
ch	chain (crochet)
cn	cable needle
cont	continue
dec	decrease
dpn	double-pointed needles
FC	front cross
foll	following
FPC	front purl cable (purl the first stitches, knit the cabled stitches)
inc	increase
k	knit
k1b/k1tbl	knit through the back of the loop
k2tog	knit two stitches together
k3tog	knit three stitches together (double decrease)

Abbreviation	Definition
kwise	knitwise (positioning right needle as if to knit)
M	marker
M1	make 1
MC	main color
p	purl
p bar inc	purl into front, then back of same stitch to increase
p2tog	purl two stitches together
p3tog	purl three stitches together (double decrease)
PM	place marker
PSSO	pass slipped stitch over
P2SSO	pass two slipped stitches over
pwise	purlwise (positioning right needle as if to purl)
rem	remaining
rep	repeat
rnd(s)	round(s)
RS	right side
sc	single crochet

Abbreviation	Definition	Abbreviation	Definition
sk	skip	tbl	through the back of the loop
SKP	slip 1 stitch knitwise, knit 1, pass slipped stitch over	tog	together
		WS	wrong side
SK2P	slip 2 stitches together knitwise, knit 1, pass 2 slipped stitches together over knit stitch (double decrease)	wyb	with yarn in back
		wyf	with yarn in front
		yo	yarn over
sl	slip one stitch purl-wise (unless indicated knit-wise)	*	repeat instructions from asterisk across row or for a given number of times
ssk	slip two stitches one at a time knitwise, then knit these two together through the back loops	( )	directions for alternate sizing *or* work instructions within parentheses as many times as indicated *or* additional information
st(s)	stitch(es)		
St st	stockinette stitch		

Appendix B: Yarn Information

All samples in this book are knit with the following Cascade yarns:

Name	Weight (in grams)	Yards	Type
Bulky Leisure	100	127	bulky
Cascade 128	100	128	bulky
Cascade 220	100	220	worsted
Tweed	100	220	worsted
Superwash 220	100	220	worsted
Cherub DK	50	190	sport
Cotton Rich	50	80	aran
Eco Wool	250	478	worsted/aran

Name	Weight (in grams)	Yards	Type
Pastaza	100	132	aran/bulky
Pima Tencel	50	109	worsted
Pima Tencel	100	220	worsted
Quatro	100	220	worsted

CASCADE YARNS

1224 Andover Park E

Tukwila, WA 98188

800-548-1048

www.cascadeyarns.com

Appendix C:
Sample Project Journal Page

Project: _____

Recipient: _____

Date Begun: _____ Date Completed: _____

Yarn (attach label below): _____

Where Bought: _____

Inspiration for Project: _____

Skills Learned: _____

Notes: _____

_____

_____

_____

_____

(attach photo of completed project here)

(attach yarn label here)

(slip page and marked-up photo copy of pattern into a page protector and place in three-ring binder)

Appendix D:
Bibliography and Internet Resources

BIBLIOGRAPHY

Thomas, Mary, *Mary Thomas's Book of Knitting Patterns*, Dover Publications, Mineola, NY, 1972.

Thomas, Mary, *Mary Thomas's Knitting Book*, Dover Publications, Mineola, NY, 1972.

Walker, Barbara, *Treasury of Knitting Patterns*, vols. I, II, III and IV, Schoolhouse Press, Pittsville, WI, 1998.

Zimmerman, Elizabeth, *Knitter's Almanac*, Dover Publications, Mineola, NY, 1974.

Zimmerman, Elizabeth, *Knitting Around*, Schoolhouse Press, Pittsville, WI, 1989.

Zimmerman, Elizabeth, *Knitting Without Tears*, Fireside, New York, NY, 1973.

INTERNET RESOURCES:

Craft Yarn Council of America:
www.craftyarncouncil.com
and www.learntoknit.com

Knitting Guild of America: www.tkga.com

Knit Lit: www.knitlit.com

Pine Meadow News: www.fibergypsy.com

Woolworks: www.woolworks.com

Index